Streets East of Bloomsbury

ISBN 978 0 904491 73 9

Depiction of Red Lion Street by Tallis (1838-40)

Streets East of Bloomsbury

Compiled by
Camden History Society

Edited by
Steven Denford and David A Hayes

Designed by
Ivor Kamlish

General Editor of Camden History Society Publications
F Peter Woodford

Sketch map of the area.
The walks (Routes) are numbered roughly in historical order of development.

See also back cover.

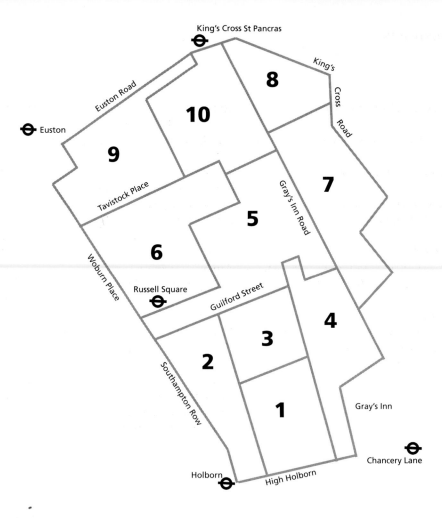

Contents

List of maps and illustrations

Historical overview

Almost all the area with which this book is concerned was once monastic land. By 1405 the monks of the London Charterhouse had come into possession of two adjoining medieval manors: **Blemundsbury** (or Bloomsbury), largely in the parish of St Giles-in-the-Fields, a narrow strip whose territory lies along our western boundary; and, to the north-east, the **Lay Manor of St Pancras**, one of several manors in a large parish extending some 4 miles northwards to Highgate. Nearer the City, and mostly in Holborn parish, was **Portpool** manor, property of the Priory of St Bartholomew, West Smithfield. By 1370 its manor house had become a 'hospitium' for lawyers, the beginnings of Gray's Inn. At the Dissolution of the Monasteries (1536-40), the property of the Priory was confiscated by the Crown and disposed of in various ways. Bloomsbury passed to the Earls of Southampton (and later, through marriage, to the Dukes of Bedford), while land ownership elsewhere in our area became very fragmented.

By the later 17th century, London's built-up area had crept north from the Thames to reach medieval Gray's Inn and the main road from the City westward now known as High Holborn. North of this, apart from a few isolated buildings, all was meadow land, where dairy cattle grazed and city folk enjoyed such pleasurable pursuits as country walks, watercress gathering, or wildfowling on the many small ponds which dotted the area – but it was a district dangerous after dark, reputedly a haunt of highwaymen and cut-throats.

The main route to the north here was Gray's Inn Lane, which at Battle Bridge (p 82), now King's Cross, crossed the river **Fleet**, the eastern boundary of the parish of St Pancras. Also known as the River of Wells, it was bordered by several 18th-century spas, two of which lay within our survey area. The locality was renowned for the purity of both its air and its water. A small tributary of the river Fleet bisected the area, running south of the line of Guilford Street before veering south-east along the course of Roger Street. This, together with various springs, served as a source for two conduits built to carry water to the City, one medieval, the other Elizabethan. The later of these lent its name to **Lamb's Conduit Fields**, a term loosely applied to the meadows stretching northwards towards the line of the present Euston Road. Reminders of both conduits will be encountered on our walks. By contrast, no trace remains of the earthworks thrown up across the local fields during the Civil War as part of the fortifications built around London to guard against a royalist attack. They ran to the north of the **King's Way**, a royal field road (the line of present Theobalds Road) used by the Stuart kings to reach the country house Theobalds in Hertfordshire.

Urbanisation of the area was slow and piecemeal, spanning more than 150 years. Plague and Fire (1665-6) forced many prosperous Londoners out of the City to live on its fringes: many gained a taste for suburban living and never returned. By the mid-1680s houses for merchants and professionals had been built at the west end of what we know as Theobalds Road. Two decades earlier, and a little further west, the Earl of Southampton, lord of Bloomsbury manor, had laid out one of the capital's first squares (now Bloomsbury Square), a move soon to be emulated inside our area by the speculative builder Nicholas Barbon. In 1684 he developed Red Lion Square, before turning his attention to two neighbouring estates – both charitable endowments: the **Bedford Charity** (or **Harpur**) estate straddling Theobalds Road, and to its north the **Rugby** school estate (*see Map 1*).

By 1720, palatial Powis House had arisen off (Great) Ormond Street, and noble Queen Square was being laid out to the west on a strip of land bordering the Bedford estate, intended to attract a more aristocratic class of resident.

Map 1. Diagram of the major estates underlying the area

St George the Martyr church, built as a chapel of ease for the new residential district, achieved parochial status in 1723, its small rectangular parish carved out of one corner of St Andrew Holborn. Eight years later St Giles, to the west, was similarly divided: the resulting new parish of St George's Bloomsbury had an irregular boundary projecting north-eastward into our area as far as its former burial ground (now St George's Gardens).

For the next 70 years the line of Guilford Street marked the northern edge of the built-up area. In 1745, new premises for the **Foundling Hospital** were built on a 56-acre field to the north. This remarkable institution occupied the site of Coram's Fields, the meadows on either side remaining undeveloped: Queen Square residents could still enjoy rural views northwards. Lending renewed impetus to the development of the area was the opening in the late 1750s of London's first by-pass, a turnpike intended to ease troop movements and allow cattle to be driven to the City markets while avoiding the congested streets of Holborn and St Giles. It was known as the **New Road** from Paddington to Islington until 1857, when the Camden section was renamed Euston Road after the Suffolk country seat of the Duke of Grafton, whose land it crossed. Ribbon development along the New Road began in the 1790s: Somers Town, built at that time to the north (and just outside our area) was, for a decade or more, indeed a distinct 'town', separated from the capital by many acres of farm land. The northward march of the metropolis had, however, already resumed. By 1790 a cash-strapped Foundling Hospital had decided to lease its spare land for house-building, resulting in the twin squares of Brunswick and Mecklenburgh, and a grid of less elegant streets nearby, in whose development the builder James Burton was a major player. An eastward extension of Guilford Street across the Doughty estate spurred Henry Doughty to complete the development of his property begun decades earlier by his forebears.

Infill from Tavistock Place to the New Road was under way by c.1807, when Burton leased land on the **Skinners'** estate, which stretched from Burton Street to Tonbridge Street, and was vested in the Skinners' Company as trustees for Tonbridge School (Kent). To the east was the small **Lucas** estate, on which Cromer Street had been begun in 1801. To its south, Regent Square was laid out in 1822 on land owned by the brickmaking **Harrison** family. Immediately south of King's Cross, and the last part of our area to be developed (1824-40), was the portion of the **Battle Bridge** estate round Argyle Square, where house building was completed only after the demise of the over-ambitious Panarmonion project (p 103).

Meanwhile, south-east of Battle Bridge, building had begun as early as 1767, encouraged by the advent of the New Road, and resulting in a little Georgian suburb centred on Britannia Street. To the south, the land sloped steeply down from Gray's Inn Lane to the banks of the Fleet. Here, east of the Lane, was the estate of Lord **Calthorpe**, part of old Portpool manor, which underwent a mixture of residential and industrial development from about 1810, the predominant builder here being Thomas Cubitt.

Our area was at first almost wholly residential. Lying on the Bloomsbury borders, it has long attracted artists, writers and intellectuals of all kinds, often while young and making their way in the world, though some settled (and died) locally after finding fame or fortune. The 19th century saw the transformation of the area into the very mixed one it is today. Various light industries colonised streets near the main roads and the valley of the Fleet. Printing and metalworking were among the district's staple industries, as were the making of scientific instruments and plaster figures, both occupations associated with the Italian community. Italians arrived in London in two phases – political exiles, usually middle-class, at the time of the Napoleonic Wars, followed later in the century by poor economic migrants from the depressed Italian countryside. Poverty and affluence coexisted cheek by jowl. By 1850 many of the mews areas and lesser streets had declined into slums, some to be replaced later by model dwellings for the 'deserving poor', or 'chambers' and 'mansion' flats for the rather better-heeled.

The railway revolution brought three main lines south to termini on Euston Road, encouraging a proliferation of hotels, both large and small, in several parts of our area. Many houses became offices, lawyers in particular favouring the streets near Gray's Inn, while trade unions were attracted to the area south of King's Cross. Numerous charities (many devoted to the welfare of women or children) established headquarters locally, in an area which had at its centre, in the Foundling Hospital, the world's first secular philanthropic corporation – a locality which Robert Louis Stevenson once described as "made for the humanities and the alleviation of all hard destinies". More houses were constantly being taken over by institutions, medical, educational or religious, some being later demolished to make way for purpose-built premises, the cluster of hospitals in and near Queen Square being a good example.

In the Second World War (WWII) few parts of this district went wholly unscathed: witness the large number of buildings under 50 years old. Three thousand bombs, largely incendiaries, fell on Holborn, taking 426 lives and destroying a seventh of the borough's buildings. Among the areas worst affected was the western end of Theobalds Road, where devastation was total; further north, the neighbourhood south of King's Cross was also badly hit. The areas of greatest destruction subsequently underwent major redevelopment, with social housing in some places, office blocks in others. The University of London continued its expansion eastward into the area, which underlies several of its institutes and student halls of residence. The streets that survived the war were in a sorry state, through damage or neglect: "grimy" and "sordid" typify the language used by writers in the 1950s to describe what are now some of the capital's most agreeable streets. It is pleasing to witness the effects of several decades of restoration, regeneration and gentrification, and to note a trend towards conversion back to residential use of many houses that were made into offices over a century ago.

Finally, the streets south of King's Cross station, until quite recently forming a notorious red-light district with numerous seedy hotels, have changed considerably. This is due both to community action funded by groups like the King's Cross Partnership

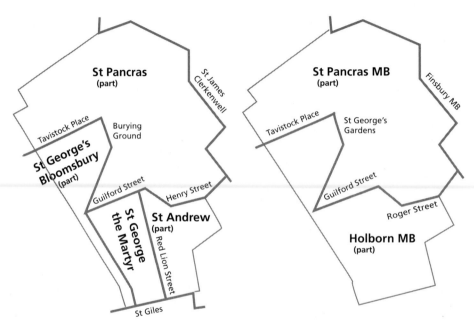

Map 2 Parishes before 1899.

Map 3 Metropolitan Boroughs, 1899-1964.

and to the knock-on effects of major urban regeneration schemes, notably the transformation of St Pancras station and the ongoing redevelopment of the former railway lands just outside our area. The administrative changes from parish vestries to Metropolitan Boroughs are shown on Maps 2 and 3 above.

Present street names and their origins

† = no specific local connection

Acton
Underlying field was
Acton Meadow

Ampton
Suffolk country seat
of Calthorpe family

Argyle
Unknown; possibly
after Dukes of Argyll

Barbon
Dr Nicholas, C17
property speculator

Bedford
Local land endows charities
in the town

Belgrove
Variant on earlier 'Belgrave'

Bernard
Sir Thomas, FH vice-
president, 1806-1810

Bidborough
A village near
Tonbridge (q.v.)

Birkenhead
Arbitrary replacement
of earlier 'Liverpool'

Boswell
Edward, a St Giles
carpenter

Britannia
Patriotic name

Brownlow
Elizabeth (fl.1675)
married into the
Doughty family

Brunswick
Caroline of, wife of
Prince Regent

Burton
James, speculative builder

Calthorpe
Aristocratic family, owners
of part of Portpool manor

Cartwright
Major John, the
'Father of Reform'

Catton
Charles, heraldic painter,
of Gate Street, Holborn

Cockpit
Site of cockfighting venue

Coley
Henry (1633-c.1695),
astrologer, of Baldwin's
Gardens, Holborn

Colonnade
Originally a colonnaded
shopping parade

Compton
Samuel Compton Cox,
FH treasurer 1806

Coram
Captain Thomas, father of
the Foundling Hospital (FH)

Cosmo
Cosmo, 3rd Duke
of Gordon, whose
granddaughter
Georgina married the
6th Duke of Bedford

Crestfield
Incomplete anagram
of earlier 'Chesterfield'

Cromer
Was Lucas Street;
James Lucas's family
hailed from Norfolk

Cubitt
Thomas, master
builder (1788-1855)

Dane
A St Clement Danes
parish charity owns
land locally

Dombey
The novel *Dombey
and Son*; Dickens
lived nearby

Doughty
Henry, of Bedford
Row, wealthy local
landowner (fl.1792)

Drake
Unknown

Duke
4th Duke of Bedford
(d.1771)

Eagle
C18 tavern and brewhouse

Emerald
Variant on earlier 'Green'

Euston
Suffolk seat of Dukes
of Grafton

Field
Surname of a landowner
or builder?

Fisher
Sir Richard, C17
local landowner

Flaxman
John (1755-1826),
local sculptor

Fleet
River (now sewer)
forming Camden's
eastern boundary

Frederick
Forename of 4th & 5th Barons Calthorpe

Gage
Unknown

Gloucester
Duke of, son of Queen Anne, convalesced locally

Gough
Richard, wool merchant, part owner of Portpool manor

Gray's Inn
Inn of Court, Holborn

Green
Unknown

Grenville
Lord, Foreign Secretary 1791-1801

Guilford
Lord North, Duke of Guildford (sic), FH president, 1771

Handel
Georg Frideric, composer, FH organist and benefactor

Harpur
Sir William, benefactor of the Bedford Charity

Harrison
Family of farmers and brickmakers, turned builders

Hastings
Sussex coastal town †

Heathcote
Michael, FH governor, 1810-1813

Henrietta
Wife of Sir Stephen Gaselee (d.1838), FH vice-president

Herbrand
Arthur Russell, 11th Duke of Bedford, 1st Mayor of Holborn

Hunter
John, physician and FH vice-president 1803-1816

James
James Burgess, associate of George Brownlow Doughty

Jockey's
Local field had various equestrian associations

John
John Blagrave, carpenter to the Doughty family

Judd
Sir Andrew (d.1558), founder & benefactor of Tonbridge School

Kenton
Benjamin (1719-1800), vintner & FH benefactor

King's
Mews off Theobalds Road, once a private royal field road, the King's Way

King's Cross
A C19 monument to George IV stood at the junction

Kirk
Sir John (1847–1922), secretary of Ragged School Union

Lamb's Conduit
Water supply to the City, financed by William Lambe

Langton
Arthur Langton Nurses' Home (Royal Free Hospital) adjoined

Lansdowne
William Petty, Marquis of Lansdowne, prime minister 1782-83

Leeke
Unknown

Leigh
Village near Tonbridge (q.v.)

Long
Descriptive

Loxham
Unknown

Mabledon
Place near Tonbridge (q.v.)

Marchmont
Hugh Hume (1708-94), Earl of Marchmont, FH governor

Mecklenburgh
Queen Charlotte, daughter of the Grand Duke of Mecklenburg-Strelitz

Midhope
Unknown

Millman
Sir William, C17 resident & developer

North
Directional

Northington
Robert Henley, Earl of,
C18 Lord Chancellor

Orde Hall
John, member of Holborn
District Board [of Works]

Ormond
1st Duke of Ormonde,
royalist Civil War
commander

Pakenham
A Suffolk seat of the
Calthorpes

Pentonville
Islington suburb developed
by Henry Penton, MP

Phoenix
Street arose 'out of the
ashes' of a local dust heap

Powis
William Herbert,
2nd Marquis of,
built Powis House

Princeton
Variant on earlier Prince's

Procter
Bryan Waller (alias Barry
Cornwall), poet and
Holborn-based lawyer

Queen
Anne

Red Lion
Nearby High Holborn
tavern

Regent
The Prince Regent, later
George IV

Richbell
John, speculative builder

Roger
Arbitrary substitute
for 'Henry'

Rugby
Local land endows
Rugby School

Sage
Frederick & Co.,
shopfitters based
in Gray's Inn Road

Sandland
Unknown

Sandwich
Kent Channel port †

Seaford
Sussex coastal town †

Seddon
Seddon family, furniture
makers

Sidmouth
Lord Sidmouth,
prime minister, and
FH vice-president
1802-44

Southampton
Earls of, C17 lords of
Bloomsbury manor

St Chad's
St Chad's Well, C18
watering-place

Swinton
James and Peter,
bought part of the
Calthorpe estate for
building

Tankerton
Kent village; East End
Dwellings Co. were
mortgagees of property
there

Tavistock
Marquess of, title of heirs to
the Bedford dukedom

Thanet
Area of East Kent †

Theobalds
Hertfordshire mansion
& hunting park
of the Stuart kings

Tonbridge
The Skinners' estate
endows Tonbridge School

Wakefield
Nearby Pindar
of Wakefield public house;
or Wakefeld Lodge,
Northants. (see p 66)

Wells
Bagnigge Wells, C18 spa

Whidborne
Rev. George Ferris,
made land available
for building Holy Cross
church

Wicklow
Unknown

Wren
Sir Christopher,
architect, sometime
Bloomsbury resident

Red Lion Square and the Harpur estate

Circular walk from Holborn station
(see back cover for map)

Begin this circular walk by walking eastwards from Holborn Tube station along High Holborn. Cross at the first set of lights and continue along the east side of **PROCTER STREET**. Created in 1961-62 as part of a new one-way traffic system, this was named after Bryan Waller Procter (1797-1874), the Holborn-based lawyer better known as the poet Barry Cornwall. The street is both lined and spanned by **Procter House**, originally built by Dynely, Luker & Moore but largely unoccupied for many years. In 2002 it was remodelled as three separate properties, reclad with an aluminium frame, stainless steel and glass curtain walling. On the east side of the street is **Eagle House**, a mixed development of small shops and offices. Opposite, to the north of Procter House, is Cycle Surgery, a large running-gear and cycle shop, while between Catton and Fisher Streets (pp 23-25) is **Lion Court**, home to the Holborn Dental Centre and the National Housing Federation.

Take the second turning right into one of London's oldest squares. It was in **RED LION SQUARE [1]** that development of our area began in 1684, thanks to Dr Nicholas

Barbon, an unscrupulous surgeon turned speculative builder. He had been baptised Nicholas Unless-Jesus-Christ-Had-Died-For-Thee-Thou-Hadst-Been-Damned Barbon and like many Nonconformists had attended university in Holland. He took a large part in the rebuilding of London after the Great Fire, within a year of which he instituted a new system of fire insurance. He set about developing a 17-acre green-field site in Red Lion Fields, which took their name from an ancient tavern in High Holborn. His initiative provoked a violent response from the gentlemen of neighbouring Gray's Inn. Incensed at the loss of their rural views, 100 of them descended on the site, and a pitched battle ensued between them and Barbon's workmen, with bricks as missiles. Unabashed, and defying legal bids to stop him, the doctor proceeded with the building of the square. It was known initially as Fisher's Walks, after Sir Richard Fisher from whom Barbon had leased the land. Seven short streets or passageways radiated from the square's corners and sides. A short-lived obelisk in the centre of the gardens commemorated Oliver Cromwell and his fellow regicides Ireton and Bradshaw. Tradition has it that their bodies were brought to rest in nearby Red Lion Yard (off High Holborn) after being disinterred from Westminster Abbey, and before being dragged through the streets to Tyburn for public exposure on a gibbet.

Watch-houses, demolished by Act of Parliament in 1737, stood at each corner of the square. Early opinions on the development were mixed: "a pleasant square of good buildings between Holborn south and the fields north", wrote one observer; "the most desolate square in London", complained another. Among its 18th-century residents was John Wilkes, renowned as an MP and radical publisher, who was Lord Mayor of London in 1774-5. In April 1769, Dr George Armstrong founded London's first public dispensary for the relief of the 'infant poor' in the home of Dr John Monro at No.7 (on a site now covered by the Procter Street roadway); the following October, the dispensary moved to East Street (p 20).

Cross over to the gardens and begin an anticlockwise circuit of the square on the surrounding pavement. On the south side, Procter House North has supplanted former No.10, for over a century home to the Royal College of Veterinary Surgeons, now removed to Mayfair. On the corner is the waggishly named **Square Pig and s'wine** bar. **Summit House**, next door, was built in 1925 as the headquarters for the tailoring company Austin Reed. Designed by Westwood & Emberton, this Art Deco period piece features glazed

1 An early depiction of 'Red Lyon Square', looking south towards Lee (now Dane) Street; bottom right, Orange Street (see p 25)

pale buff tiles arranged in vertical bands to accentuate the building's steel frame; other attractive decoration is provided by railings with lotus leaf motifs, and carved panels on the entrance doors, by Percy Metcalfe. Planning permission for the dark brick extension behind (in Dane Street) to house clothing collections was given on 1 September 1939, but such development was prevented by WWII.

Nowadays, the building houses the law firm Mishcon de Reya. A blue plaque on the side wall of Summit House recalls the residence on the site, from 1752, of John Harrison (see also p 25), whose perfection

of the marine chronometer was eventually recognised as providing the most accurate way of determining longitude at sea, and financially rewarded only three years before his death at No.12 in 1776, on his 83rd birthday. The site was later occupied (until 1923) by St Paul's Hospital for Skin and Genito-Urinary Diseases.

Across Dane Street (p 23) is red-brick Victorian Halsey House. Arnold Bennett stayed at a friend's flat here in 1902, the year in which *Anna of the Five Towns* appeared. No.13, on the site, had earlier housed the offices of the Mendicity Society (see p 42). Although the square suffered grave bomb damage in 1941, four original terrace houses survive beyond, built by Barbon c.1686 and re-fronted in the early 19th century. At No.16 was the Hospital for Women, founded in 1842 by the obstetrician Dr Protheroe Smith (1809-1889), who pioneered the use of chloroform in childbirth. The hospital opened its doors to patients in January 1844 as the Hospital for the Diseases of Women, "exclusively for the reception and treatment of females who are afflicted with diseases peculiar to the sex". It was the first of its kind in the world. Demand was such that it moved out to larger premises in Soho Square in 1852. **No.17** was home in 1851 to the painter Dante Gabriel Rossetti, required by his landlord to keep his models "under some gentlemanly restraint, as some artists sacrifice the dignity of art to

the baseness of passion". The same house in 1856-59 was shared by the painter Edward Burne-Jones and the wide-ranging William Morris, cared for by a housekeeper nicknamed 'Red Lion Mary'. An LCC plaque dated 1911 recalls the residence of all three artists. In 1861 the celebrated firm of Morris, Marshall, Faulkner & Co. was founded at No.8 (back on the site of Procter House North), with a kiln in the basement for firing tiles and stained glass.

The painted brick-faced flats of **Brampton** and **Culver House** stand in the south-east corner of the square, where Red Lion Passage, a preserve of publishers, once ran off diagonally, just as Lamb's Conduit Passage still does from the north-east corner. We will come across more of this 1950s development by Holborn Metropolitan Borough Council in Red Lion Street. To the north of Princeton Street **Tresham** flats occupy the site of the office of the Sheriffs of Middlesex, and of No. 23, where in 1798 died the much-travelled Jonas Hanway, founder of the Marine Society and a benefactor of the Foundling Hospital; he is also remembered as the first man to carry an umbrella.

On the north side of the square, **Conway Hall** (1929, in grey brick and by F H Mansford, Waterhouse's chief draftsman) is home to the South Place Ethical Society, named after its original location in Finsbury. Founded in 1839 by Moncure Conway, a liberal Christian, it became

agnostic 30 years later, but its winter programme of Sunday chamber music concerts, which began in 1887, continues a long tradition of permissible Sabbath-day activity. An anti-fascist demonstration outside the hall in 1974 turned into the notorious Red Lion Square Riot, in which Warwick student Kevin Gately died, prompting an inquiry by Lord Scarman.

Rose-tinted **New Mercury House** (built in 1980 for but no longer occupied by Cable & Wireless; see also Mercury House, p 18) stands on a site occupied at various times by a Jewish school, the Trinitarian Bible Society, the British Asylum for Deaf & Dumb Females, the Home for Penitent Women, and the University Tutorial College, where H G Wells once taught. No.28 was home in 1928 to actress Fay Compton. No.31 in 1854 saw the foundation by F D Maurice of the Working Men's College, soon to move to Great Ormond Street (p 34).

Beyond Old North Street is **No.34**, with a plain, narrow front of hammered concrete decorated with dividers and T-square. This was formerly offices for the architects Seiferts. **Churchill House** at No.35 is the headquarters of the Royal College of Anaesthetists, but was built in 1956 by Lander, Bedells & Crompton as offices for the publishers Cassell's. Sir Winston Churchill, one of their authors, laid the foundation stone. The firm relocated to Westminster in the early 1980s, taking with them a reclining statue of the native-American princess Pocahontas, which had become a well-known feature of the square.

To compensate, over at the east end of **Red Lion Square Gardens**, is a bust by Marcelle Quinton of the philosopher Bertrand Russell, who lectured at Conway Hall. It was unveiled by Mrs Dora Russell in 1980. A seat in front commemorates local WWII hero Alfred Wilson aged 38 of 16 Red Lion Passage, killed while on active duty with the London Heavy Rescue Service on 16 October 1940, along with five colleagues and 17 civilians following air raids on St Alban's Buildings, Baldwin's Gardens. At the western end of the gardens is a small 1985 statue by Ian Walters of the pacifist Fenner Brockway, which after damage in the great storm of 1987, was reinstated in 1988 by Irene Chamberlain and others in memory of W J Chamberlain and all opponents of war, and also of Joan Hyams. Nearby, a Golden Indian Bean tree was planted in memory of Alistair David Berkley, a law lecturer at the Polytechnic of Central London, who died on Pan Am 103 at Lockerbie on 21 December 1988. In the early 1990s, the gardens were re-landscaped by Charles Funke Associates.

Long-lost No.1, on the west side of the square, was the London Dispensary for Diseased and Ulcerated Legs, founded in 1857 under the auspices of Florence Nightingale. The following year No.4 witnessed an early demonstration of refrigeration by engineer James Harrison. St John the Evangelist, a beautiful 1000-seat church **[2]** designed by J L Pearson, and erected by Dove Brothers for total cost of £22,836, dominated this side of the square from its consecration in 1878 to its destruction in 1941, after which its ruins faced what had by then become the Bloomsbury trolleybus terminus. Not everything was lost in the air raid: some decorative features from St John's went to St George's Bloomsbury, while a fine chandelier by Ninian Comper now graces All Hallows Church, Twickenham. On the site today is the large 1961 block, currently Central St Martin's (p 25) Department of Industrial Design, but previously occupied by other academic institutions: Westminster University's School of Law, formerly part of the Polytechnic of Central London, and earlier the LCC's Holborn College of Law, Language & Commerce, itself a merger of two institutions, of which Princeton College (p 22) was one.

Walk north along the side of Churchill House, where Procter Street becomes **DRAKE STREET**, all of 40 paces long. It was already bereft of its original 12 houses by Edwardian times, and much widened as part of the 1960s one-way system. Cross at the pedestrian lights

2 St John's Church, Red Lion Square (from *Building News*, 3 Jan 1879)

to arrive in front of **Transport House** (headquarters building of Unite, of which the former Transport & General Workers Union is now a part) on the north side of **THEOBALDS ROAD**. Often pronounced 'Tibbalds Road' by local people, this once formed part of the King's Way, a private field road used by the Stuart kings to reach both Newmarket and their hunting park at Theobalds in Hertfordshire. By the early 18th century, houses had been built at this western end, then known as Theobalds Row. The antiquarian John le Neve was living here in 1717 when his *Monumenta Anglicana* was published. In 1878, the carriageway was widened and Theobalds Road was integrated with its eastern continuation, until then still known as King's Road. Tramlines were laid down here by the North Metropolitan, a company operating mainly in East London. Until 1905-6 its horse-drawn cars ran from Clerkenwell and points east to a terminus at the west end of Theobalds Road. The tramway was then electrified and extended into the new Kingsway tunnel (the only central link between tramways north and south of the river), with power supplied through a conduit laid under the roadway. A new direct road link with Vernon Place and Bloomsbury Way turned Theobalds Road into the major traffic route it is today.

All but flattened in WWII, its north side hereabouts is now wholly modern, lined by post-war office blocks of 9-10 storeys.

Across Boswell Street at **No.124,** stone-faced **Mercury House** (1955) adorned by reliefs depicting the airborne messenger of the gods. The building was refurbished in 1992 as the headquarters for Cable & Wireless, who have since relocated to Paddington Basin, the advertising agency Mediacom taking its place in 2007. Set in the protruding wall to the left of the main door, at pavement level, is a tiny inscription dated 1955 and marking the historic boundary of the Bedford Charity estate, which once bisected the block. Sir William Harpur (or Harper), a man of humble birth who rose to become Master of the Merchant Taylors' Company and Lord Mayor of London, died in 1573, and left 13 acres and one rood of meadow land in 'Conduit Shott' to provide dowries for girls in his native town of Bedford, and to endow a grammar school which he had recently re-founded there. His charity became a model for subsequent merchant leaders in London to emulate, and the Bedford Charity (or Harpur Trust), with objectives to promote education, relief in sickness or need, and recreational facilities in Bedford and surrounding areas, remains one of the largest 200 charities in the UK.

After a rationalisation of boundaries with a neighbouring landowner in 1654, the Bedford Charity (or Harpur) estate comprised an L-shaped area running east from Mercury House to Emerald Street, then crossing Theobalds Road and embracing land between Bedford Row and Red Lion Street. Before 1684 the charity trustees were in negotiation with Barbon, anxious to maximise revenue, but suspicious of the shifty, near-bankrupt doctor. A complex legal wrangle was still unresolved when he proceeded to erect houses willy-nilly on both the Harpur and neighbouring Rugby estates. It is not clear how much of the area was completed by Barbon, although the street plan was certainly his; he died in 1698, ruined by a national financial crisis, leaving houses half finished. A contemporary account compared one uncompleted street to the "ruins of Troy".

Mercury House stands on the site of the Harpur Arms, which until c.1913 had boasted a galleried yard of the kind now seen in London only at the George in Southwark. Next door was a luxurious picture-house, one of the first in Britain with an American-style soda fountain. Opened in 1922 as the Bloomsbury Victory cinema, and later renamed the Bloomsbury Super, it evolved into a news theatre before suffering a direct hit in WWII.

Eastward formerly stood two large red-brick office blocks thrown up by the Government in 1948-50, and condemned by Nikolaus Pevsner as "crushingly utilitarian". Ariel House, for the Ministry of Civil Aviation, later became Adastral House of the Air Ministry, its new name coined from the motto of the RAF.

Lacon House beyond, built around three sides of a courtyard – which until their demolition in 1953 contained Nos.82&84 – was originally occupied by the Board of Trade. Both blocks were in use by the MOD until its mass exodus to Bristol c.1996, after which they were demolished and replaced by brick-and-glass office blocks of somewhat less boring appearance. Cross New North Street to look at **No.98**, the Adastral House replacement, now occupied by the film company MGM. Hogwarts school and house shields in the foyer announce their association with the Harry Potter films. The second block, beyond Harpur Street, housing the law firm Nabarro Nathanson, has retained the **Lacon House** name. Among the buildings lost on this side of Theobalds Road in WWII were the White Horse pub at No.98 and the Cross Keys at No.80, a music hall of some note in 1867-87, which vied with another (the Lord Raglan) almost exactly opposite.

Look across to the south side of Theobalds Road, where some Victorian buildings escaped destruction in WWII. Standing out in pale blue, at **Nos.49&51**, are the north entrance to the Conway Hall, and the former Bradlaugh House, until recently the HQ of the British Humanist Association, and still of both the National Secular Society and the South Place Ethical Society, proprietors of the adjoining Hall. Modern blocks to the right cover the site of former No.15, birthplace in 1875 of Samuel

Coleridge-Taylor, the mixed-race composer of *Hiawatha*. His father, an African doctor, had returned permanently to Sierra Leone, probably unaware that Samuel's Croydon-born mother was pregnant.

Briefly retrace your steps to the spot opposite where **OLD NORTH STREET** emerges as the northern egress from Red Lion Square. Turn right into **NEW NORTH STREET**, its continuation. In 1753, before the introduction of house numbering, a hatter was recorded as living here at, paradoxically, the sign of the 'Golden Leg'. Nothing remains of Barbon's houses, and the later tenements of Dunstable Court have given way to the post-WWII council flats of **Springwater**, a name recalling the district's aqueous associations. The street's Victorian northern end includes a former public house at **No.18**, known for generations as the George & Dragon until renamed the Moon c.1980, and latterly an Irish 'theme pub', Murphy's Moon; change to office use was granted in 2000, residential use having been refused two years before. Opposite is a former printing works, later named Albion House, and latterly occupied by Leon Paul, the world-renowned makers of fencing swords, now removed to Brent Cross.

Here turn eastward along what was once the west end of Dombey Street, taking care not to trip on an unexpected 'sleeping policeman'. Originally part of Barbon's East Street, this is now a

footway flanked by the flats and gardens of 6-storey **Windmill** and 10-storey **Blemundsbury**, designed by Hening & Chitty, and completed in 1949 by builders William Moss & Sons Ltd of Cricklewood. Pevsner (a year later) was complimentary about these blocks: "not lavish, but of delicate precision and agreeably devoid of mannerisms ... [with] prettily detailed balconies". Although Blemundsbury (as Bloomsbury was once known) is a laudable attempt at a historically relevant name, we are here some way to the east of that medieval manor. The block covers the site of No.30 Dombey Street, in whose garden lay one of the sources of Lamb's Conduit (p 39). With a need to help local families who had lost their homes to enemy action in WWII, Holborn Metropolitan Borough Council identified the devastated area north of Theobalds Road as suitable for new housing to accommodate 4,000 people, with a shopping centre, community centre, primary and nursery schools and open spaces. The LCC, however, was opposed to any residential development in Holborn at the end of WWII.

Beyond, intersecting from the right, and separating the two large blocks in Theobalds Road, is **HARPUR STREET**. This was developed only in the second half of the 18th century, when it supplanted two earlier narrow alleyways named Theobalds Court and Bedford Court. Dr John Fothergill, a Quaker specialising in the treatment of sore throats, died in Harpur Street in 1780. The surviving **No.10** at this north end has a fine Doric portico with a broken pediment, and dates from 20 years earlier. **Bevan John House** next door looks as old, but was purpose-built as flats, and must date from a rebuilding of the street c.1883. A passageway burrows through the block into private **Harpur Mews**, once the yard of James Soanes, whose Victorian business here combined stationery supply with waste paper disposal. In the rebuilt Harpur Street, at No.18 on the west side, C McShee & Son, builders and decorators, were established in 1893. Nos.7-9 opposite were an early headquarters of the Society for the Prevention of Cruelty to Children (now NSPCC), which ran a rescue home here for badly treated youngsters. The 1922 edition of the *Holborn Official Guide* carries an advertisement for the 150-room Caledonian Hotel at Nos.1-5: "one price 5/6, no extras" for bed, bath, breakfast, etc. An earlier house on the site, at No.4, was home from 1824 to Jacob Perkins, the American banknote printer turned steam engineer, who invented the lethal (if impractical) Perkins Steam Gun.

Continue ahead along **DOMBEY STREET**, which now runs only east of Harpur Street. East Street was renamed in 1936 after Dickens' *Dombey and Son*, but although the author lived for a while in nearby Doughty Street (p 47), the novel has no particular local associations. In this still wholly residential street, **Nos.9-15** form a uniform row of handsome 4-storey houses of the early 18th century (re-fronted 1765-7), with unusually slender pedimented doorways, and basements approached by very narrow steps, all sensitively restored by the Circle 33 Housing Trust. The dignified range opposite at **Nos.18-22** was much altered in the 19th century; in recent years, the houses have been converted into flats by architects Levitt Bernstein, but preserving the early panelling in the front rooms. Set in the walls of No.22 and of its neighbour (No.2 Orde Hall Street) are boundary plaques inscribed "BCB 1883" (for Bedford Charity Bounds) and "Rugby Estate 1884".

On reaching **LAMB'S CONDUIT STREET**, pause to look right (and southward). Begun by Barbon in the 1680s, the street was for 90 years regarded as an extension of Red Lion Street (p 21). Although most of it (p 38) lies on Rugby land, its once war-torn southern end was on the Harpur estate. **Nos.21-27,** the first block on the right, built on the site of a bicycle factory, was occupied first by a firm of house furnishers, and later by Longmans the publishers. Of the many charities with headquarters locally, none was so intriguingly named as the Society for the Prevention of Premature Burial, which c.1900 occupied a house beyond, on the Lacon House site. From 1925 until it was bombed in 1940, No.15 there was home to Italia Conti's academy of theatre arts; the singing emanating from the school could be heard from the undertakers' at No.45. At about the same time, the building was also the meeting place of the Ancient Order of Druids. On the left at **No.10** is Holborn Police Station, now the Camden headquarters of the Metropolitan Police. Above it towers the 13-storey office development of the Harpur Trust that until quite recently housed the Aliens' Registration Office (now in Southwark). An earlier foreign presence on this site, at erstwhile Nos.14-18, was the business of the French Pathé brothers, later of newsreel fame, but listed in Edwardian times as makers of phonographs and "talking machines".

Now turn left along Lamb's Conduit Street (*for this stretch see p 40*), crossing over and turning right along an alleyway forming one arm of L-shaped **EMERALD STREET**. Until 1885 this was Green Street, named after Edmond Greene, the first headmaster of Bedford School, or a bowling green associated with a nearby cockpit (p 45). On the left pass at No.35 the **Bedford House Community Centre**, which is home to the Holborn Community Association. A little way farther down on the left, above the rear doors to the former French's Dairy (p 41), prominently painted "Dairy", two stones (dated 1776 and 1838) mark the Rugby/Harpur boundary. Exchanges of property between the two estates meant that the street has belonged at different times to both. Turning right, notice a further plaque, set in the wall of **Nos.26-34**, an old printing and bookbinding works: "Bedford Bounds", it declares, referring, of course, to the Bedford Charity (Harpur) estate rather than the better-known ducal demesne to the west. The north-south section of the street is lined by 4-storey factories and warehouses, products of the 19th-century commercialisation of the area, although some are postwar rebuilds. Firms noted here in the 1930s included Robert Adams at Nos.3-5, who claimed to make the world's best door springs, the 'Victor'; and Howells, manufacturers of bakers' specialities and wholesale fancy confectioners at Nos.23-29. As late as 1960, the street was home to a Christmas-cracker factory. Old taking-in doors survive in abundance, such as those at **Nos.20-24**, once a sponge warehouse, and at **Nos.11-15** and **Nos.17-21**, both former printing works. Printing has been replaced as the street's staple industry by the modern sister profession of graphic design. Little **RICHBELL PLACE**, leading off to the right, was built as a cul-de-sac in 1710 by one John Richbell; he also had a hand in the building of East (now Dombey) Street.

We re-emerge into **THEOBALDS ROAD**, alongside the **Queen's Head** pub, whose inscriptions testify to its establishment in 1812 and rebuilding 65 years later. At the time of writing it was boarded up. Turn right along Theobalds Road, whose south side opposite is lined by rather grim buildings of 1878-80, with shops and cafés at street level, some of them helpfully sporting their dates of construction and owners' initials: for instance, the letters 'FK' on several buildings must refer to Frederick Kingwell, a prominent local landlord in the late 19th century. Maybe it was to such a man that a young H G Wells paid his 4 shillings a week when in 1888 he rented an unidentified attic room in Theobalds Road, with paper-thin walls which rendered conversation impossible when traffic went by.

Turn right, past the south side of the **police station**, with its frontage of Portland stone and fortress-like slit windows on the second floor; it was built in 1962-3 by J Innes Elliott, then chief architect of the Metropolitan Police. Cross at the traffic lights to the south side of the road, noting on the corner, at **No.25**, a sign for the brass foundry of Messrs Yannedis, a long-established, now long-departed, firm of architectural ironmongers. Behind, and running diagonally through to Red Lion Square, is **LAMB'S CONDUIT PASSAGE**, a well-used footway once noted for its small jobbing printers; some of their shop fronts remain.

RED LION STREET, along which we turn southward, dates from the late 17th century, and was originally residential, attracting professional people, notably solicitors. It later evolved into a typical 19th-century 'high street' of shops and eating places (p 2). After heavy wartime damage, it is now an untidy mix of old and new, including some uninspired modern office blocks built by the Harpur Trust. A **Dolphin** tavern "in Red Lion fealds" was recorded as early as 1690. Its Victorian successor at the north end of the street was half destroyed in the first Zeppelin raid on London on the night of 8 September 1915; the clock over the bar remains stopped at 10.40 pm, the time of the raid. Opposite at No.38 is the luckier **Enterprise** (its sign a sailing ship), a 19th-century rebuild of an earlier 'Grapes'. Note, on its south-facing wall, the attractive mosaic design (by Tessa Hunkin, 2006), depicting the same ship, with a polar bear on an ice floe. The Enterprise was the first ship to search (unsuccessfully) for Sir John Franklin and his crew, who had disappeared in 1848 while trying to find the North West Passage.

On the street's west side, an Italian restaurant occupies **No.46**, one of a dozen surviving, though much altered, early houses – a reminder that the district was a hub of London's Italian community before its centre of gravity drifted eastward to Clerkenwell. Red Lion Street was once noted for its figurini and sellers of plaster casts. **No.51** was the long-time home of the Mazzini-Garibaldi Club, founded in 1861 as a facility for Italian working men. Having moved here in 1933, it was requisitioned during WWII as enemy property, but reopened in 1951. It was regretfully closed by its ageing membership in 2008.

Turn left along **PRINCETON STREET** (Prince's Street until 1885). On the south side, at the decidedly mock **Tudor House**, is the Mosaic Shop. Next door is the former Prince's Street Board School, of 1877 though entered through a curiously classical archway. The building served after WWII as the LCC's Princeton College of Language of Commerce, and until 1999 was the **Holborn Centre for the Performing Arts**, part of Kingsway College, when the building was converted into self-contained flats. Opposite stands a modern block housing the Inns of Court School of Law, with a car park in what was once Dog & Duck Yard. Turn right at Bedford Row, the eastern boundary of the Harpur estate. Although most of the west side belongs to the Bedford Charity, and its estate office was once at No.26, much of the Row belonged to the Doughty family and their forebears, and we shall return to it in Route 4 (p 43).

For the moment, take the next right turn into **SANDLAND STREET** (known as Bedford Street until 1878), where the **Old Nick** on the north side is a c.1900 building. This was until recently the Three Cups, descended from a tavern built on Charterhouse land and recorded in 1472 as the 'Three Cuppes'. The frontage of the pub follows the line of Gray's Inn Passage, which once struck diagonally north-westwards to join with Red Lion Passage **[3]** in providing a now lost pedestrian route through to Red Lion Square. Through an archway, **Three Cups Yard** became a gated housing development connected with the former performing arts centre. The opposite side of Sandland Street is the rear of the early-21st-century massive grey metal and glass **MidCity Place,** at No.71 High Holborn. This supplanted the huge block named State House (housing government offices such as DHSS and the Patent Office), whose 1950s ground-breaking design had been much praised by Pevsner.

Pause at the corner of **RED LION STREET,** to look along its south end. **Nos.68-70** (formerly New Century House, named after the cleaning company once based there), was refurbished at the turn of the millennium with a new glazed façade and a lopsided canopy entrance; the building that stretches into Eagle Street is occupied by the BPP Law School. Beyond are Seifert's self-effacing **Lion House,** and the defiantly ugly **Allied Dunbar House.** On the far corner is the **Old Red Lion,** a 19th-century incarnation of the ancient inn which gave the street its name. The 'Old' prefix was possibly added

3   Red Lion Passage [1922]
(drawing by Alan Stapleton)

to distinguish this pub from a later one, at Nos.62-63 Red Lion Street, called the Red Lion and Ball. Behind you on the corner is **No.20**, a 1950s building, given a pleasing new cladding of dark blue glass in the mid 1990s. Opposite, mulberry-painted **Hyltons** (No.56A) and **Beaconsfield** (No.64) are further examples of Holborn Borough Council's post-war housing, this time low-rise flats with small shops beneath, and as Pevsner/Cherry notes, "scaled to fit".

Now cross over and continue ahead along **EAGLE STREET**, one of the area's oldest streets and once one of its poorest; its atmospheric, and in places ruinous, streetscape was all but obliterated in bombing raids of April and May 1941. In the first half of the 20th century, this street's trades supplied the needs of central London businesses, with such firms as the New Century Cleaning Co., building contractors Mullen & Lumsden, specialist printing and stationery supplier the 'Nig' Manufacturing Co., and door furniture and wholesale hardware suppliers G & S Allgood. A much earlier trade was frame making, by Elizabeth and Thomas Jupp in the 1790s. Martin van Butchell, born here c.1770, became a successful, if eccentric, quack doctor with a waist-length beard, who rode the West End streets on a spotted pony. Today almost all the buildings post-date WWII. The **Finnish Institute**, an appropriately Nordic building at Nos.35-36, stands

on the site of the 18th-century Eagle brewhouse, demolished in 1793. Note the elephant plaque, high up on the façade, its significance a total mystery. Templar House covers the site of the popular Royal (or Holborn) Amphitheatre, which flourished until bomb-damaged in February 1941. On the north side, the Leukaemia Research Fund (**Nos.39-40**), the Sierra Leone High Commission (**No.41**), and the Folio Society's headquarters (**No.44**), typify the range of offices in smaller central London streets at the turn of the 21st century. The modern pub/brasserie the **Bountiful Cow** was formerly the Overdraught and is housed in the ground floor of **Beckley** flats.

Cross over short **DANE STREET**, leading north into Red Lion Square, and so named since 1907. Originally Leigh (or Lee) Street, it later merged with Dean Street, its southward continuation (now buried beneath 1950s Sunley House, with its 1990s glass makeover). Here in the 19th century was a blacking factory. 'Dane' is a variant on the earlier street name. Land here has been owned since 1522 by the 'Holborn Charity' of the parish of St Clement Danes at the Aldwych. Passing **Yorkshire Grey Yard** (right), a diminutive, now unlabelled, access road recalling another lost pub, emerge into Procter Street, from which you may return to Holborn Underground, also the starting point for Route 2.

From the King's Gate to Queen Square

Linear walk between Holborn and Russell Square stations
(see back cover for map)

From the main (Kingsway) exit from Holborn Underground station, walk north towards Southampton Row. At the crossroads glance east along the north side of High Holborn to determine the spot where former Kingsgate Street (see below) once emerged, the gap filled nowadays by a McDonald's at No.112. Crossing High Holborn, and keeping on the east side of Southampton Row, pass the blackened baroque façade of the **Baptist Church House** of 1903, designed by Arthur Keen, a pupil of Norman Shaw. The Baptist Union has now moved out of London, leaving behind a statue of John Bunyan (by Richard Garbe), set in a corner niche at first floor level, and accompanied by the opening words of *The Pilgrim's Progress*. Planning permission was granted in 2008 to convert this building into a hotel.

The Church House turns the corner into **CATTON STREET**, which was the western end of Eagle Street (p 23) until severed from it in the 1960s by Procter Street. Charles Catton (1728-98) was a heraldic painter of Gate Street, Holborn. On its

south side, surmounted by a cupola, is **Kingsgate House**, formerly part of Kingsgate Baptist Chapel, originally founded in 1736 as the Particular Baptist Church, Eagle Street, by Andrew Gifford, its pastor until his death in 1784. Joseph Ivamy was another notable minister there from 1805, and one of the first co-secretaries of the Baptist Union from its formation in 1812. The chapel was twice rebuilt, latterly in circular form. It once stood on the corner of Kingsgate Street [4], where Dickens has Mrs Gamp (in *Martin Chuzzlewit*) lodging, next door to the mutton pie shop and opposite the cats' meat warehouse. This north-south thoroughfare, obliterated in 1902-06 by the LCC's Kingsway scheme, followed the line of the old royal highway already mentioned (p 18), which here ran north out of (High) Holborn to join what is now Theobalds Road. At the south end stood a barrier called the King's Gate. Here in 1669, wrote Pepys, the royal coach was overturned, depositing Charles II and his companions in the road – a case, however, of 'all dirt and no hurt'. (A reminder of the King's Gate is Gate Street which winds its way, just south of Holborn station, from Kingsway into Lincoln's Inn Fields.)

Two left turns lead us into short, featureless **FISHER STREET**.

4   Kingsgate Street before demolition (print dated 15 Dec 1902)

24

Sir Richard Fisher owned the land here in the 17th century. It once housed on its south side St John the Evangelist School and a generating station of the Metropolitan Electricity Supply Co., designed so that its huge working dynamos could be admired from the pavement: the humming metal panels of today's substation are a poor substitute. The street's north side would have been dominated by the vast Church of St John the Evangelist, but post-war redevelopment leaves us with an unattractive modern annex of Central St Martin's main building, which we come to shortly.

Fisher Street debouches into **SOUTHAMPTON ROW**, the north end of Edwardian Kingsway in all but name, which recalls the eponymous Earls, 17th-century lords of Bloomsbury manor. It absorbed the earlier, narrower, King Street. To our left, at Nos.8-10, is **Carlisle House**, originally a hotel and offices of the Royal London Friendly Society. It was built by Bradshaw, Gass & Hope in 1905-06 in grandiose Edwardian style faced in Bath stone and renovated in 1997 after years of dereliction. On the ground floor is the **Ivy House** pub.

Turn right. Across the roadway is the northern portal of the Kingsway Tram Subway, closed in 1952, and since variously used as a film set, as a control centre for London's flood defences, and to store traffic signs. Tramlines remain set in the cobbled incline. We walk alongside the Central School of Arts & Crafts, founded by the LCC in 1896 and moved here from Regent Street twelve years later. It was built 1905-08 by the LCC Architects Department under W E Riley, but with much input by the School's first principal William R Lethaby, who is commemorated by a blue plaque. Lethaby requested that the building should be "plain, reasonable and well-built". It blends granite and Portland stone to interesting effect, and granite columns surmounted by carved capitals are a feature of the interior, for example in the exhibition space. The School is now known as the **Central St Martin's College of Art & Design** (part of the University of the Arts London). However, the School is to be relocated to the Granary Building north of King's Cross in 2010. An offshoot of the school, adjoining it around the corner, is the (Jeannetta) **Cochrane Theatre** of 1963. It covers the site of Holborn Fire Station, a 4-storey gabled building with a tower. In the 1901 census, 13 households and 69 residents, 19 of them firemen, were recorded as living there.

Notice how the north façade of the art college tucks itself in behind the theatre, following the line of erstwhile Orange Street, once another of the short diagonal approaches to Red Lion Square. The horologist John Harrison settled here in 1735, soon after his arrival in London from Humberside to promote his prototype 'H1' chronometer, and stayed here for 17 years before moving to Red Lion Square (p 14). The street was renamed Parton Street in 1860. No.4, before WWII, was a celebrated left-wing bookshop run by David Archer. Nearby, on the corner of Drake Street, were the publishers Lawrence & Wishart. After the demise of the tram, and the closure of the Kingsway tunnel in 1952, Parton Street formed part of the terminal loop used by trolleybuses from the east.

Cross to the north side of Theobalds Road, where the **Grange Holborn Hotel** has been remodelled from a post-war office block; another office block, now Transport House (p 18), has extinguished the former White Hart pub on the corner of Boswell Street, which had been rebuilt on its original site after wartime destruction. Turn left along **OLD GLOUCESTER STREET**, dating from the early 18th century, and named after the Duke of Gloucester, longest-surviving son of Queen Anne, who unlike his sixteen even sicklier siblings lived to the ripe old age of eleven, having spent time in our locality to benefit from the purity of the air. On the west side, 1930s style **Faraday House** survived incendiaries in April and May 1941 (which obliterated neighbouring properties to the south), possibly because of its steel framed construction. To its north, many old houses were spared, too, including **No.44**, with a plaque commemorating the death here in 1781 of the 90-year-old Bishop Richard Challoner, Vicar Apostolic to London's Catholics at a time of great bigotry against them. The previous year, during the Gordon Riots, ruffians called at No.44 to find that their prey had fled an hour before. An earlier Gloucester Street resident was Robert Nelson. He was a 'nonjuror' (one refusing to swear allegiance to William III), who was a founder member of both the Society for Promoting Christian Knowledge and the Society for the Propagation of the Gospel. In 1822 the charismatic Rev. Edward Irving stayed at No.19 on first arriving in London, in what he called "good, elegant rooms" in an "airy and healthy" area. Edward Fitzgerald (p 62) lived at No.15 in 1854.

More old houses, at **Nos.32-26**, face the secluded **Alf Barrett Playground**; named in memory of the chairman of the Tybalds Close Tenants' Association, who lived in Blemundsbury (p 19) from 1973 until his death in 1990. He campaigned for council homes for young couples and single homeless people, as well as for a children's playground – which did not open in his lifetime. Incidentally, the estate's name was coined by Camden Council because nearby Theobalds Road is often pronounced "Tibbalds" by local people. The sculpture by Maria Debra Solway of Humphry, the Mary Ward Centre's house cat (named presumably after Mary's husband), was originally unveiled in its

former Queen Square location in 1997.

On the opposite side, reached through an archway, is **No.27**, a former factory which made motor accessories in 1907. The company British Monomarks was established here in 1925, as the metal sign declares. It operated in tandem with the Post Office to provide companies with a 'monomark' which, stamped upon goods, stood for the company's full name and address. It now provides virtual office services, including PO Box number hire and mail forwarding.

At the north end of the street are the old St George the Martyr schools, now united in John's Mews (p 45). They have had a complicated history since 1708, when a school for 20 boys and 20 girls was established in the church's Vestry House. The boys moved to Cross (now Gage) Street in 1739, and on again in 1852 to the south side of Theobalds Road, their place in Cross Street being taken by the girls and infants who had meanwhile remained at Vestry House. A new building for 200 girls and 200 infants opened in 1863, in what is now called **Lundonia House** (incorporating the **October** (art) **Gallery**) at No.24 on the east side of the street. When Theobalds Road was widened in 1878, the boys moved back to new premises next door to the church – "ugly and gloomy Gothic" was Pevsner's verdict on this S S Teulon creation, now occupied by private-sector Jeff Woolner College.

Retrace your steps and turn east along very narrow and mainly pedestrianised **GAGE STREET** (Cross Street until 1894), which runs alongside the playground. On the left at the far end, before WWI, stood the Brown Bear public house. Turn right into **BOSWELL STREET**. It dates from the 1690s, and was originally known as Devonshire Street, hence modern **Devonshire Court** on the east side above shops. Turn right and pass **Cecil House**, built to house homeless single women by Cecil House (Inc), which was founded by Mrs Cecil Chesterton, wife of G K Chesterton's brother Cecil, in 1926. Beyond **Bevan House** we reach the south end of the street where two similar brick and concrete blocks of flats face each other: **Richbell** and **Falcon**. The latter block, on the west side of the street, lies on the site of Devonshire House, which predated the street. The 3rd Earl of Devonshire had the house built in 1668 for his son, William Cavendish, who was at the time MP for Derby and eventually became 1st Duke of Devonshire in 1694. Cavendish lived at Devonshire House for 15 years, subsequently moving to Montagu House (the site of the British Museum). He gave evidence on behalf of Lord Russell who had been implicated in the Rye House Plot, and also held secret meetings in the cause of William of Orange. The house was then leased to the widow of Richard Leigh of Lyme Park (Cheshire), who lived there until her death in 1727, aged 85. Thereafter, until the early 20th century, the house suffered a decline, finishing up with as many as five living in one room – not uncommon for houses in this street. In 1934, Devonshire House was purchased by Major Benton Fletcher to house and open to the public his collection of furniture, paintings, virginals and harpsichords; in 1937 it was presented to the National Trust. The house was destroyed in WWII, but the instruments had already wisely been evacuated to Fenton House, Hampstead.

Before he was twelve, the poet Alexander Pope (b.1688) underwent part of his erratic schooling in Devonshire Street at the mercy of a master whom he described as a "Popish renegade". No.29 was home from 1828 to William Brockedon, the artist, author and inventor, whose *Passes of the Alps* inspired Murray to publish his well-known Guides. Harold Monro ran a poetry bookshop at No.35 from 1913 (formally opened by Henry Newbolt) until 1926, when it moved to Great Russell Street, finally closing in 1935. One of Monro's first customers was Alida Kiernantaski, who ran the business from 1916 when Monro was called up, and married him in 1920. Charlotte Mew first visited the shop in 1915, and the poet Robert Frost took rooms above it in 1913 "by pure accident". A painting room in Devonshire Street was rented in 1928 by Victor Pasmore, a co-founder of the Euston Road school of painting.

Right up to WWII, many poor Italians – organ grinders, ice cream vendors and chestnut sellers – lived in the street, alongside a small colony of workers in gold, aluminium and brass. In the 19th century the Italian patriot Giuseppe Mazzini is thought to have lived here for a time. He spent many years of exile lying low, quietly (and ineffectively) plotting the overthrow of Continental autocrats. Ever cosmopolitan, Boswell Street today is almost wholly lined by 20th-century blocks of flats housing a high proportion of Bangladeshi residents.

Retrace your steps towards the north and make a quick detour into paved **BOSWELL COURT** (right). The footway was named, not after Johnson's biographer, but after Edward Boswell, a St Giles bricklayer and churchwarden who built houses here; the court lent its name to the adjoining street when the latter was renamed (from Devonshire Street) in 1937. The blue-and-white building on the left was, in 1906, a factory making upholsterers' trimmings and bag frames. It faces the flats of **Boswell House**, bearing railed walkways.

Now continue along Boswell Street, past nondescript **ORMOND CLOSE** which once led through to Little Ormond Yard (p 41), and reach tranquil **QUEEN SQUARE**. You may wish to sit on one of the benches under the trees, while we consider the square's history. Built in 1706-20 on land owned by Sir Nathaniel Curzon of Kedleston, it was designed for the sons

of the Duke of Devonshire and known at first as Devonshire Square, though soon renamed in honour of Anne, the reigning queen. Originally aristocratic, it was home in 1728 to a peer and three bishops (of Carlisle, Chester and Chichester), and by mid-century to five peers of the realm. Artists and intellectuals later colonised the square, but very few of their houses remain, most having been rebuilt, or replaced in the 19th century by hospitals, convents or places of education. Windsor lamps atop the lamp-posts lend an air of antiquity to the Square, as does the cast-iron pump in the paved-over roadway at this south end, where maids once would have queued to fill their jugs and pails. Early on, the houses were not numbered. One early resident was Elihu Yale, Governor of Madras and of the East India Company, who bought a house in the Square in 1710 or 1711; he also had two houses in Southampton Row. He amassed a great collection of paintings and other treasures, most of which survived a disastrous fire in 1719, then to be sold at a series of sales two years or so later. He eventually gave part of his library to a collegiate school in New Haven, Connecticut – known today as Yale University.

From the top of Old Gloucester Street we start on an anticlockwise tour of the square. In a house here on the south side, the music historian Charles Burney lived in 1771-72. His daughter Fanny [5], whose

novel *Evelina* would appear in 1776, wrote of the "beautiful prospect" from the house "of the hills, ever verdant and smiling". (The north end of the square had been left undeveloped to preserve the view northward, an amenity lost when the Foundling estate was built up.) The Burneys' visitors included Garrick and Goldsmith as well as Captain Cook, who dined here just before leaving on his second voyage of discovery, accompanied by Burney's son James. Charles' musical interests lived on in the

square in the shape of the Queen Square Select Society, devotees of Beethoven during the composer's lifetime. Richard Limpus, who founded the Royal College of Organists in 1864, lived at No.41.

No.42 (once two imposing 18th-century houses), is now the bustling **Mary Ward Centre** for adult education and community advice, removed here from Tavistock Place (p 63). The building previously housed evening classes of the ILEA's Stanhope Institute, the former LCC Technical School for Women, whose curriculum included dressmaking, millinery and photography; and, before WWI, the Government School of Art for Ladies. Earlier still it was a temporary home of the College of Preceptors, founded in 1846 as an examining body for teachers. Next door is the former Italian Hospital, opened in 1884 by Giovanni (John) Ortelli in his own house, No.41, with a largely Italian-speaking staff to serve his poorer immigrant countrymen. It later expanded into No.40 and a house round the corner in what is now Boswell Street. In 1898-99 a new building was erected, designed by T W Cutler in a Renaissance style, with a fine cupola topped by a gilded cross. The Boswell Street extension was built in 1911 by J D Slater. Falling demand for beds led to the discharge of the last patient in 1989. Still boldly inscribed with the hospital's name, and with a version of the Italian royal arms above its door,

the building is now the **Italian Wing** of the Great Ormond Street Hospital.

Ignoring the west wing of the Homeopathic Hospital (p 34), walk north along the east side of Queen Square. Its Georgian houses (quite differently numbered from the present houses) have all given way to later buildings. An early resident on the east side of the Square was the portrait painter and author Jonathan Richardson the elder (1667-1745), a close friend of Alexander Pope, whose family sat for portraits by him. The younger Richardson (1694-1771) listed in the 1750 Rate Book, was a portraitist of limited capacity, being very short sighted. Thomas Morson (senior, 1800-74) was established as a retail pharmacist in Southampton Row at the age of 21, branching out into pharmaceutical manufacture in Hornsey Road and later Ponders End; he was a founder member of the Pharmaceutical Society, and later as President. He died at his home, No.38.

At No.37, completed by the building firm Dove in 1921, was the head office of the National Deposit Friendly Society, designed by W H Ansell of Ansell & Bailey. The Society had been founded by Rev. George Raymond Portal, who had been a curate in Pimlico and had witnessed the horrors of slum life, but was against public and private charity. The NDFS was the first friendly society to discuss old age pensions, and to build and own a convalescent home.

The Portland stone building was damaged by bombing in WWII.

A survival until 2005 (and last domestic building to have remained on the Square's east side) was diminutive Grade-II-Listed No.33, which had been sandwiched endearingly between its bulkier neighbours. It was occupied by St Katherine's Convent, run by an Anglican sisterhood which was noted for its School of Ecclesiastical Embroidery. In 1909 the sisters converted to Catholicism and decamped to Farnborough Abbey (taking with them the original chapel altar). The glass-fronted structure (nearing completion in 2008) at **No.33** is for a new clinical neuroscience building. Former No.31 housed the Aged Poor Society, and the Society of St Vincent de Paul (named after the patron saint of charitable institutions), which once supplied the nursing staff for the Italian Hospital. At No.29, a house noted for its elaborate decoration, was the Working Women's College, founded by Elizabeth Malleson in 1864 after she had failed to persuade its male counterpart to admit females. Ironically, her own establishment was to become co-educational ten years later as the College for Men & Women, under which name it closed in 1901.

The mid-19th century saw the closure at former No.24 of a very different female education establishment, namely a prestigious private academy founded in the 18th century, and nicknamed the 'Ladies' Eton'. Here Veronica Boswell, daughter of James, was among the pupils of the redoubtable Mrs Sheeles; as was Fanny Burney, whose father Charles taught at the school for some 15 years. The girls worshipped at St George the Martyr, travelling the few yards to the church in a decrepit old carriage in order to practise getting in and out with due decorum. When the coach could no longer be moved, it was set up within the academy so that the girls could continue their lessons in propriety. It was *im*propriety that led to the sacking of the satirical poet Charles Churchill, a tutor at the school. Jerome K Jerome later lived in Queen Square for a while, probably at No.29, though the humorist himself could not be sure, having had "no head for numbers". Female education of a third kind took place at No.22, home in 1858-63 of the Ladies' Charity School previously in John Street (p 48), which trained poor girls for domestic service.

In 1865 'The Firm' (Morris, Marshall, Faulkner & Co), founded by William Morris and others in Red Lion Square, moved to No.26, with workshops in a converted ballroom at the rear. Morris, weary of daily commuting from the wilds of Kent, moved into the house with his wife and children. Although he wrote here his *Earthly Paradise*, he would not have described the square as such, for he never enjoyed living here, and in 1872 moved with his family to west of Hammersmith. His by then flourishing business stayed at No.26 for a further nine years before relocating to Merton Abbey.

All these houses gave way to what is now called the **National Hospital for Neurology & Neurosurgery**. It was founded in 1859, on the initiative of the Chandlers, a middle-class St Pancras family whose grandmother had suffered a stroke, with support from David Wire, then Lord Mayor of London, and himself the victim of a minor neurological attack. Originally the National Hospital for the Paralysed and Epileptics, it later became the National Hospital for Nervous Diseases. Opened at No.24 with just eight beds for females, it soon expanded into neighbouring houses. Purpose-built accommodation followed in 1885, when the Albany Memorial Wing was erected, in red brick and terracotta to the design of J W Simpson of Manning & Simpson. Known for a time as the 'Albany Memorial', it bears a stone in memory of Leopold, Duke of Albany. The plain extension of 1937 (by Slater, Moberly & Uren), on whose balconies patients could take the air, was financed by public subscription, but named the Rockefeller Wing after the American foundation which sponsored the hospital's research. There is a foundation stone laid by Princess Alice of Athlone, longest surviving granddaughter of Queen Victoria, and reliefs (by Arthur J Ayres) affirming the institution's dual

30

objectives of 'research' and 'healing'. Pioneering the active treatment of nervous disorders, the National rapidly gained an international reputation, and has since expanded to take over a considerable proportion of the square.

A footway leading from its north-east corner into Guilford Street is known today as **Queen Anne's Walk**. Beside it looms the 10-storey concrete block of the **Institute of Neurology** (1970-78, by Llewelyn-Davies & Weekes), the sickly brutalism of its exterior scarcely conducive to nervous composure. A more elegant predecessor on the site was Queen Square House **[6]**, a substantial mansion of 1779 with a large projecting portico facing west. It could have been here that George III was rumoured to have stayed (p 32) "in a ground floor room overlooking Guildford Street". Baron Pollock, Lord Chief Justice, lived here in 1844-62. The mansion then served until 1899 as the English Presbyterian theological college (previously at No.29 Queen Square). It subsequently housed the Jews' College until 1932, when it was converted into single-room flatlets "for ladies". (The Jews' College moved to Woburn House in Upper Woburn Place and is now in Hendon, renamed

the London School of Jewish Studies.) In 1948 the Foundling Estate surrendered the lease to the National Hospital, and the house was subsequently demolished in spite of a preservation order; the discovery that its porch dated only from 1830 had supposedly weakened the case against its destruction.

Until 1794, the north side of the Square was open towards countryside, but soon thereafter the rural view was blocked by the houses of Guilford Street. The flats of **Queen Court** were built in the 1930s. The German scholar Mary Wilkinson (1909-2001) lived at Flat No.33 after her retirement from University College in 1976. Next door, at **No.23**, are the former headquarters and laboratories of the Royal Institute of Public Health & Hygiene (founded 1931), whose name is still prominently inscribed. Beyond is another footway leading out of the square into Guilford Street, past a small garden and an entrance to the underground car park of the President Hotel.

We however continue south along the west side of the square. Here Robert Louis Stevenson and his wife Fanny set the house of Harry Desborough in *The Dynamiter* (1885), their convoluted fictional tale of 19th-century terrorism. Real-life No.21 was home in 1846-56 to the Dissenting theologian and social reformer F D Maurice, the founder of Christian Socialism and of the Working Men's College (p 37).

No.20 was the house of Dr John Campbell, to which Dr Johnson repaired on a Sunday evening for conversation, though troubled by the "shoals of Scotsmen who flocked about". Later occupants included Edmond Hoyle, the 18th-century expert on whist; Louisa Twining, the poor-law and workhouse reformer, who raised eyebrows by sheltering homeless women in her house; and the architect Thomas Wyatt. By 1907 No.20 had become a Quaker institute. Accessed through a trap-door in the back garden were the stonework tunnels of the second source feeding a medieval conduit we shall encounter again later in Rugby Street (p 40). Known initially as the Devil's Conduit (diabolic names were given to anything novel or strange), and by the 18th century as the Chimney Conduit (after the shape of the conduit head), it survived until 1911-13, when the house was replaced by Turkish baths for ladies. These in turn were demolished c.1960. In adjacent Queen Square Place, built a few years later than the square on land owned by the Earl of Salisbury and originally named Brunswick Row, two lords and a general once lived as neighbours. It is now only the goods entrance of Russell Square's Imperial Hotel.

Alexandra House is at No.17, once the Alexandra Hospital for Poor Children with Hip Disease. As the House of Relief for Children with Chronic Disease of the Joints, it was founded in 1867 to meet a

6   Queen Square, looking south from Guilford Street; porticoed Queen Square House on the left (R Ackermann, 1 Sep 1812)

problem then prevalent in working-class children. The present building, by Marshall & Vicars (1899), served the hospital for 21 years until it moved to Swanley (and subsequently to Luton in 1940). It later housed a Fighter Control Unit of the Royal Auxiliary Air Force, before conversion to offices in 1960. It is now part of UCL's Institute of Cognitive Neuroscience.

Though much altered, 18th-century houses survive at **Nos.14-16**, the latter a home for working boys c.1907-25. **St John's House** at No.12 (architect Eustace Frere) was a base for the sisterhood of St John & St Thomas, an Anglican nursing order, which in 1906 moved into Queen Square from Norfolk, bringing their 50-year-old convent with them. Individually numbered stones are said to have been used to erect a replica of their former premises. St John's House later served as a home for night nurses at distant St Thomas' Hospital. It was taken over by the National Hospital in 1967, and renovated in 1995 as a functional imaging centre. Carefully preserved are reliefs depicting an eagle, and a snake in a chalice, both symbols of St John, as well as a small statue of the evangelist with a tiny version of the cupped serpent in his hand.

Imposing, red-brick **Nos.8-11**, designed by Andrew Prentice in a somewhat French style, were built in 1909 as joint examination halls of the Royal Colleges of Physicians and of Surgeons, a role which lasted until the 1980s. Now named **Sir Charles Symonds House** (after an ex-president of the Association of British Neurologists), and part of UCL, the coats-of-arms of the two Royal Colleges still adorn the façade. It is the base of the Wellcome Trust High Field Magnetic Resonance Laboratory Imaging Centre. In 1865-73 former No.8, on this site, housed Dr Williams's Library of nonconformist literature, now in Gordon Square. It was the birthplace in 1842 of the traveller and author Janet Ross (née Duff Gordon).

No.7 and **No.6** are two 18th-century survivals. Since 1913 the latter has been the headquarters of the Art Workers' Guild, founded in 1884 by a merger of two groups of young artists, whose members included W R Lethaby and Walter Crane. In 1914, the Design and Industries Association was founded at No.6, with the object of preaching the gospel of 'fitness for purpose' as applied to all industrial art. The same year, the architect Cecil Brewer and his family moved to the house when the Smith & Brewer practice also relocated there. The building provided London offices for the Spiritualist Alliance and its library of psychic literature; lectures by leading spiritualists Sir Arthur Conan Doyle and Rev. Vale Owen were held in the Arts Workers' Guild Hall, "looked down on" by the busts of leading AWG Masters. The site of No.5, home to the National Pharmaceutical Union until the 1950s, is covered by **No.3**, modern headquarters of the publishers Faber & Faber, whose concrete and glass is out of character with everything else in the square. **No.2**, by contrast, is of the later 18th century and has an attractive iron balcony. The **Queen's Larder** pub at No.1 dates, as a building, from c.1710. There is a story that George III once stayed in the square for private treatment by his physician, and that his devoted wife Charlotte rented a cellar here, under what was then an unnamed beershop, to store culinary delights for his comfort. Evidence for the King's stay is unfortunately both scant and inconsistent.

Queen Square Gardens, maintained by Camden, are open to the public by agreement with the Council, but closed for one day each year to maintain their private status, as evidenced by the badges of the National and children's hospitals which each surmount one of the gateways. At the south end, a floral bowl celebrates the Queen's Silver Jubilee of 1977, as do lines by Philip Larkin and Ted Hughes set in the paving alongside. Nearby, "Sam" the cat, sculpted by John Fuller, was unveiled in 2002, to commemorate his owner Patricia ("Penny") Penn; she championed conservation in the locality, being active in the Rugby and Harpur Residents' Association. Another resident of Holborn, Margaret Louisa Rowland (1899-2003), is remembered with a bench in the south-east corner. Two benches commemorate the death of 16 homeopathic doctors in the Trident air disaster of 1972, while another remembers Nazy Mozakka, a biomedical scientist at Great Ormond Street Hospital, who died in the London bombings on 7 July 2005. Set in a circle of crazy paving in the lawn north-east of the central pathway is a small plaque marking the spot where a bomb landed during a night-time Zeppelin raid in 1915, without loss of life even though 1,000 people were asleep in their beds around the square at the time. During WWII twice that number slept in a shelter under the gardens. In the centre of the gardens, at the spot vacated by Humphry the cat (p 26), there is now a bronze by Patricia Finch depicting a mother and child, unveiled in memory of Andrew Meller in 2001, and purchased by the friends of the children of Great Ormond Street Hospital.

At the north end of the gardens is the lead statue of a queen, erected in 1775 and paid for by Mr Oliver Becket, a resident. The subject's identity is controversial. Caroline and Mary II have been suggested as (unlikely) candidates, but the Victorians believed her to be Anne. The modern consensus, as a plaque indicates, is that despite her archaic dress she is Charlotte, consort of George III. In his *London Statues*, Arthur Byron unkindly concludes that "the face of the statue is pretty, which should eliminate them all, especially Charlotte".

At the south-west corner of Queen Square is the church of **St George the Martyr**, predating the actual square, and built by private subscription in 1706 as a chapel of ease to St Andrew's Holborn for the residents of this then new suburb. The builder was Arthur Tooley. In 1718-20, it was repaired by Nicholas Hawksmoor. In 1723 it was promoted to parochial status, and an early rector was William Stukeley, an antiquarian whose (erroneous) theories on Stonehenge earned him the nickname of 'Arch-Druid'. In 1868 the originally plain church was radically altered by S S Teulon, who plastered its walls, and replaced its previously squat bell tower with a curiously shaped zinc-clad steeple; carved symbols of the four evangelists occupy circular niches in the east wall. St George's is sometimes known as the "sweeps' church", because of the annual Christmas dinner provided there by Captain James South's Charity for 100 chimney sweeps' apprentices, until the use of climbing boys was outlawed in 1875. The poets Ted Hughes and Sylvia Plath were secretly married at the church on 16 June 1956.

COSMO PLACE is a lively footway leading west to Southampton Row. Catering largely for the inner man, it offers two restaurants, and two pubs of some antiquity, the **Swan** dating back to at least 1757. The paved western end lies just within the Duke of Bedford's Bloomsbury estate, hence its name; the granddaughter of Cosmo, Duke of Gordon married into the Russell family.

It was called Fox Court until renamed in 1858, and then merged in 1885 with the cobbled eastern part, originally known as Little Ormond Street. The Bloomsbury Park Hotel covers the site of two Georgian houses called Rector's Glebe, as their rents were paid to the incumbent of the neighbouring parish church. Their ground floors were eventually converted into shops; it was above a baker's at No.12 that conductor (Sir) John Barbirolli was born in 1899 of Italian-French parents. A blue plaque in his honour faces the main road, into which we may turn right to walk north to Russell Square and its Underground station (second turning on the right). Alternatively, return to Queen Square for the start of Route 3.

Mostly the Rugby estate

Circular walk from Russell Square station
(see back cover for map)

In 1567, a field named Conduit Close was donated to Rugby School (Warwickshire) by its founder, Lawrence Sheriff. Although it has disposed of many freeholds over the years, the school still owns much property in this locality, and the Rugby estate is the subject of most of this circular walk from Russell Square station. Turn left from the station, then left again along Herbrand Street and, crossing Guilford Street, turn left and follow the first pathway opposite, just past the President Hotel, into Queen Square.

Bear left and at the far (south-east) corner of the square, turn left into **GREAT ORMOND STREET**, and pause on its north side. Dating from the 1680s, the street named Ormond Street until 1885 when it merged with New Ormond Street, its easterly extension, and was radically renumbered. James Butler (1610-88), 1st Duke of Ormonde, had been a royalist commander in the Civil War and later Lord Lieutenant of Ireland.

18th-century Ormond Street was a very desirable address, the sizeable houses on its north side having had very long gardens backing onto open country. Residents included Robert Nelson, the philanthropist and religious writer whom we met in Old Gloucester Street; Henry Vansittart, a future governor of Bengal; and Martin Folkes, the antiquary and natural philosopher. With similar interests was William Stukeley (also p 33), who lived here 1717-26; a friend at the time of Sir Isaac Newton, he was the first to record the latter's tale of the falling apple. Another Ormond Street resident was Charles Jennens, one of Handel's librettists, who compiled the text of *Messiah* from selected Scriptural extracts. Lord Thurlow, a widely unpopular ("vulgar, arrogant, profane and immoral") Lord Chancellor, was living at erstwhile No.45 in 1784, when thieves broke into his study and made off with the Great Seal of England; never recovered, it had to be remade. Thomas Babington Macaulay, also a lawyer, but better known for his historical works, lived from 1823 at old No.50, the home of his father, the slavery abolitionist Zachary Macaulay. No.49 was home to Dr Richard Mead (1673-1754), a royal physician of international repute, chief physician to the Foundling Hospital (p 50), great collector of works of art, and patron of artists.

As the gentry migrated westward, institutions moved in. Almost all of these establishments are long gone, but two hospitals remain. At the north-west end of the street, where we are standing, is the **Royal London Homeopathic Hospital**, administered today by the UCL Hospitals NHS Foundation Trust. Its royal prefix was added by command of George VI. Founded in 1849, in Golden Square (Soho), the hospital moved ten years later into a house in Great Ormond Street. The purpose-built premises of 1893-95 were designed by W A Pite, with a curious jumble of motifs. The more harmonious Sir Henry Tyler Wing (1909), on the corner of Queen Square, was the work of E T Hall. He also designed the red-brick former nurses' home on the opposite side of the road, now connected with the street's other medical establishment, the world-famous **Great Ormond Street Hospital** (GOSH). The building now houses the innovative Paul O'Gorman Patients' Hotel, which accommodates GOSH patients and their families. Adjacent is the new-built **Weston House** (by Anshen + Allen Architects), named after the Garfield Weston Foundation, a longstanding supporter of GOSH. Paul O'Gorman died of leukaemia, aged 14, in 1987. Before he died, he made his parents promise to help other children suffering from the disease. When Paul's sister Jean also soon died of cancer, Diana, Princess of Wales, was instrumental in founding the charity Children with Leukaemia (p 37).

Look left down **POWIS PLACE**. Separating the two hospitals, and now little more than an ambulance road, this

Powis House in Ormond Street

occupies the site of palatial Powis House **[7]**, built in 1705 for William Herbert, the 2nd Marquis of Powis, who was once sent to the Tower as an alleged Jacobite sympathiser. His mansion later became the French embassy, but burned down in 1714, possibly as a result of arson. Louis XIV paid for its reconstruction, which wisely included a water reservoir on the roof, doubling as a fishpond. Ironically, in view of Herbert's sympathies, his house was later home to Philip Yorke, the 1st Earl of Hardwicke, who presided as Lord High Steward at the trials of the Jacobite lords in 1745, sentencing many of them to death, and who later banned the wearing of the Stuart kilt. After his death there in 1764, Powis House became the Spanish embassy. Soon after 1783, it was demolished, and a street of attractive smaller houses was built on the site. Only two of them survive, along on the left at **Nos.2&3**. In the 1850s, the politician Peter Alfred Taylor (known as PAT), kept open house for leading radicals at his home in Powis Place. At about the same time, John Leech, the caricaturist, *Punch* contributor and friend of Thackeray, was living at No.6, next door to a home for 'friendless girls'.

At the bottom of the long garden of Powis House, on the banks of the Fleet tributary, were Powis Wells, an extensively patronised but never fashionable spa, complete with pump room and pleasure gardens. Its buildings were later converted into a sanatorium for sick children at the Foundling Hospital (p 50). Here today is GOSH's 8-storey Southwood Building, erected in 1938 with Stanley Hall as architect, and named six years later after Lord Southwood, the hospital's late chairman.

Known until recently as the Hospital for Sick Children, GOSH was founded in 1851, when most hospitals granted admission to young children only exceptionally. One, for example, admitted under-sevens only for amputations. Dr Charles West, with some colleagues, rented Dr Mead's old house at No.49 and opened with just 10 beds in 1852. Six years later, No.48 was acquired, and a new Gothic building, designed by Edward M Barry, was started in 1872, covering the long back gardens of the two houses. It opened five years later, and was followed by a new south wing in 1893. A proposal to relocate the hospital to the Foundling Hospital site had foundered for lack of finance at the time of the Depression. All subsequent development has perforce been concentrated on this constricted island site north of Great Ormond Street. Such expansion and reconstruction have been helped by J M Barrie's well-known gift to the hospital in 1929 of all royalties from performances of *Peter Pan*. These it continues to receive, thanks to a special dispensation in the 1988 Copyright Act promoted by former prime minister Lord (James) Callaghan. On the right-hand side of Powis Place is the Variety Club Building (by Powell & Moya, 1994).

Facing **GREAT ORMOND STREET** is a fragment of the original Barry edifice, in vivid red brick, now renamed the Paul O'Gorman Building. Beyond it is the canopy of the hospital's new main entrance. Turn left under the canopy to view, on the left near the entrance, the bronze figure of Peter Pan, sculpted by Diarmuid Bryon O'Connor and unveiled by Lord and Lady Callaghan in 2000, whose ashes were scattered in the little garden surrounding the statue after their deaths in 2005. Peter wears a scarlet cloak and lighting on his finger is a tiny Tinker Bell, added by O'Connor in that year and unveiled by Sophie, Countess of Wessex. Preserved at the heart of the modern complex is E M Barry's original hospital Chapel, a domed neo-Byzantine extravaganza with stained glass by Clayton & Bell, an alabaster reredos and child-size pews. It was transported intact to its new site on a concrete platform.

Return to the street, cross to the south side and continue east. Nos.41-61 form a continuous row of surviving houses, which some believe may have been started as early as 1686 by Dr Barbon. No.57 was home in the early 1960s to the architectural critic Peter Fleetwood-Hesketh (1905-85), who was then Secretary to the recently formed Victorian Society, to which he offered an office here. The Society held its board meetings in **No.55** next door. There in 1877 William Morris had founded the Society for the Protection of Ancient Buildings (SPAB). Morris and his wife Jane had lived, as newly-weds in 1859, at old No.41 on the other side of the road, while awaiting completion of their 'Red House' at Bexleyheath. In the same year Philip Webb, architect of the Red House and Morris's friend, set up his own practice at No.7 (now **No.59**). SPAB were at No.55 until May 1983 when they moved to Spitalfields. The building was subsequently home to the League of Remembrance. **No.51** houses the offices of the charity Children with Leukaemia, mentioned earlier. **No.49** has an attractive doorway, and a wooden front that is probably a product of its late-Victorian role as a coffee tavern. A 3rd-floor flat at **No.45** was home for half a century to the novelist, biographer and critic Vincent Brome, until his death in 2004. **No.43** now houses the Cardiovascular Sciences Unit of the Institute of Child Health. The entrance to **No.41** is a splendid creation with Ionic demi-pilasters and a florid surround. The house was occupied in 1915-39 by the West Central Collegiate School, a long-surviving superior 'dame school' previously in Mecklenburgh Square (p 56).

Opposite, GOSH's plain pale-brick Frontage Building was completed as a new Outpatients' wing after WWII. On this site, in 1857 the Working Men's College moved from Red Lion Square (p 14) into Lord Thurlow's old house at No.45, later expanding into No.44 next door (formerly a Dressmakers' & Milliners' Home), before moving on to Crowndale Road in 1906. F D Maurice (p 31), the first principal, was succeeded by Thomas Hughes, author of *Tom Brown's Schooldays*. Eminent lecturers included Ruskin, Darwin and T H Huxley, while E M Forster (p 60) ran a weekly Latin class. The Catholic Church of St John of Jerusalem adjoined, at Nos.46-47, the RC Hospital of SS John & Elizabeth, founded in 1856 by Cardinal Wiseman to serve the sick poor. Old No.40, on the north side, was home for many years to the Lincoln's Inn & Temple Choir School. Otto Weber, the painter and engraver, died at No.32 in 1888. No.36, for several decades, housed the offices of stained-glass painters Burlison & Grylls. No.38 was where the novelist and painter Wyndham Lewis set up his short-lived Rebel Art School in 1914. Some original houses beyond were replaced by Victorian 'chambers' blocks: Ormond and Garden Chambers, and Norton Chambers, home in the 1890s to William Archer, the Scottish drama critic and translator of Ibsen.

Intersecting from the right is Orde Hall Street (p 41). Demolished to make way for it was old No.25, home to the novelist Harrison Ainsworth on his arrival from Manchester (c.1824) for legal training in the Temple. More early houses remain at **Nos.19-27**, with two agreeable Victorian shop fronts. 19th-century No.19 and Georgian Nos.21-25 (with later fronts) were renovated c.1993 for the Rugby estate by Lander Associates. **No.27** once housed the UK Benefit Society, founded in 1828; ninety years later rooms here were rented by Saxon Sydney-Turner, Treasury mandarin and shadowy member of the Bloomsbury Group. A blue plaque at **No.23** identifies the home (1777-90) of the prison reformer John Howard, who inherited the house from his sister; he was, however, travelling widely in Britain and Europe at the time, comparing penal systems. **No.21** has been the home since 1998 of High Stakes, which claims to be the UK's leading gambling bookshop.

The post-WWII GOSH School of Nursing has been replaced by the hospital's 2006 **Octav Botnar Wing** (Anshen + Allen Architects again), opened by the Prince of Wales and the Duchess of Cornwall. Romanian-born, Botnar came to Britain in 1966 speaking no English. Making a fortune selling Datsun cars, he eventually became the billionaire head of Nissan UK. In his lifetime he quietly donated some £100 million to charity. In 1991 he fled to Switzerland, and from a police investigation into alleged tax fraud involving the Camelia Botnar Foundation, a charity to benefit disadvantaged young people founded by Octav and his wife in 1978 after the death in a car crash of their daughter Camelia. (Always protesting his innocence, Botnar was still suing the Inland Revenue for malicious prosecution when he died in 1998.)

Continue ahead across Lamb's Conduit Street (p 39) into what was originally New Ormond Street. Several 4½-storey houses here date from 1710-20. Faced with a huge maintenance bill for the large number of Grade-II-Listed buildings it owned, most occupied by tenants paying low, controlled rents, the Rugby estate sold 42 of the houses in this part of the street to Camden Council for rehabilitation. Camden acquired **Nos.1-17** (right) in 1974, for repair by Donald Insall & Partners; original panelling and staircases were preserved. Nos.9-15 were partly demolished as dangerous structures, and rebuilt with replica façades, No.11 replete with a fine porch. A plaque on **No.13** dated 1980 commemorates the restoration. The economist John Maynard Keynes, another of the Bloomsbury Group's less artistically inclined members, lived at **No.10** (left) in 1914. **Nos.4&6** housed the family and business of James Cockle (d.1854), apothecary and vendor of the 'family anti-bilious pill'. The list of 200 celebrity customers that he inserted in each pillbox included seven dukes and two successive prime ministers; Charles Dickens also took the pills, mentioning them in his letters.

Reaching Millman Street, glance to the right. Observe how the dog-leg at the top, where Great James Street begins, is labelled

MILLMAN PLACE, always its official designation. Turn left along **MILLMAN STREET** itself. Its southern end was begun c.1690, on the Rugby estate, by Sir William Millman. Settling here in 1720 was the eccentric dissenting clergyman John 'Orator' Henley, whose later Oratory was in Clare Market (Aldwych) and who famously described the English politics of his day as "a Hanoverian Pig-stye". In 1812 John Bellingham, a disgruntled Liverpudlian bankrupt, lodged in the street before making his way to the lobby of the House of Commons to assassinate the prime minister, Spencer Perceval. Neo-Gothic architect S S Teulon lived at erstwhile No.18 in 1841; and Gerald Brenan (also p 44) lodged at No.10 when he first arrived in London and took to writing.

Lining the street's east side today are modern flats clad in red hard brick, with Soane-like blank entrances. They were built by Farrell & Grimshaw for Camden Council in 1974, after the original east-side terrace collapsed. On the west side stand two Council-restored Victorian terraces dating from 1888, as the small plaque on **No.25** attests. The northern end of the street (once New Millman Street) was completed only in 1803, and lay on the Foundling estate, into which we now briefly stray. An early resident was the transvestite Chevalier D'Éon **[8]**, sometime soldier, diplomat, master swordsman and secret agent of Louis XVI. Disabled by

a wound sustained in a fencing accident, he spent his twilight years at No.26 New Millman Street in the guise of a woman. When he died in poverty in 1810, and his body was medically examined, neighbours were astonished to learn that the person they knew as the "Chevalière" was really a man. Past **Millman Court** flats is **MILLMAN MEWS**, on the left, a cul-de-sac leading only to what was once the Doughty Garage. Opposite, the yellow-brick sheltered housing of Shan House – **Nos.52-58 MILLMAN STREET** – was built for Camden by Hunt Thompson Associates in 1991-92. Two early houses survive at **Nos.60-62**, with later **Coram Mansions** beyond**.**

Turn left along Guilford Street, and shortly left again through Guilford Place (p 53), to reach the north end of **LAMB'S CONDUIT STREET**. Here, on the corner of the **Lamb** public house are parish boundary marks, "SPP" for St Pancras, into which former parish we have fleetingly trespassed; and "SAH" for St Andrew Holborn, which we now re-enter. Dating from c.1779, the pub was once known as the Lion & Lamb. Its Victorian incarnation was well restored in 1961, the fine tiled front and suspended lamp, internal woodwork and engraved glass, and the 'snob screens' at the bar being retained. The pub also boasts a working music-hall 'Polyphon' which can be played in aid of charity. The sculptor Jacob Epstein once frequented the Lamb,

8   The Chevalier D'Éon de Beaumont,
'from the original',
published by R S Kirby,

as did various members of the Bloomsbury Group. In Virginia Woolf's *Jacob's Room*, the eponymous habitation is either in or very near Lamb's Conduit Street.

Glance into the mews area known as **LONG YARD**, which was originally longer, extending through to Millman Street. **Nos.4-5** once housed a cab and coach builder, and a farrier. By the yard entrance, set in the wall of modern **Rokeby House**, is a stone structure inscribed as follows: "Lamb's Conduit the Property of the City of London this Pump is Erected for the Benefit of the Publick". In 1577 William Lambe **[9]**, a wealthy member of the Clothworkers' Company, paid £1500 for the renovation of an old conduit house at Snow Hill dating from 1498. Lead pipes were laid to bring water there, by way of Leather Lane, from a dammed Fleet tributary and from some of its associated springs. It was here near Long Yard that the water was captured for use by local people and a pump was provided by the public-spirited City fathers, possibly fed from a reservoir rediscovered in 1851 in the cellar of former No.88 Lamb's Conduit Street. Although the importance of the conduit diminished when the New River was opened in 1613, many people compared the purity of the local water favourably with that of the Hertfordshire commodity. Rebuilt in 1736, the conduit survived only a further decade before demolition. The stone effigy of a lamb

9   William Lamb(e); published 1782 by Richard Godfrey

which had adorned the conduit head later served as the inn sign of the Lamb tavern. Today, the ram trademark of Young's brewery is, confusingly, more in evidence.

On the opposite side of **LAMB'S CONDUIT STREET**, at old No.42, the publisher Sampson Low began business in

1819 as a bookseller and stationer; attached to his shop were a circulating library and reading-room frequented by many literary men, lawyers, and politicians. The former No.43 was the birthplace in 1772 of Thomas Underwood, the painter and geologist, a proprietor in 1800 of the newly formed Russell Institution (p 61). His subsequent detention in France during the Napoleonic Wars led to the unique eye-witness account of the Siege of Paris in his *Journal of a Détenu*. By 1900, No.95 had become the National Vaccine Establishment for Vaccination Direct from the Calf, later the Animal Vaccine Lymph Station. On the site today are GOSH's 4-storey, brick-built **Camelia Botnar Laboratories**, whose controversial development in 1993-95 (by DEGW) was conditional on renovation of the façade of Listed **No.83** next door, previously Mel Calman's Cartoon Gallery and now adapted as the Paul O'Gorman Research Centre.

On the next left-hand corner is Starbucks; its opening in 2006 was unsuccessfully opposed by those fearing that the street's character was under threat. The **Perseverance**, diagonally opposite, was from 1995 an Irish 'theme pub' (the Finnegan's Wake), but was traditionally known as the Sun and, though much altered, dates from the early 19th century. Continue south to the next crossroads. The mostly pedestrianised central section

of the street retains something of a 'high street' atmosphere, though many shops supplying everyday needs have given way to more specialised and up-market outlets. Eating places spill on to the pavement, lending a Continental air to what has long been a cosmopolitan area. The Conduit Coffee House (right), otherwise Sid's, was for generations a café run by the Italian Domenidietti family. Opposite, at **No.64**, a dated inscription flanking a 'bundle of fasces' motif, recalls the founding in 1843 – in North Gower Street – of the United Patriots National Benefit Society, one of six similar bodies created in the earlier 19th century to provide sickness cover and life assurance for ordinary people. An archway (now gated) next to No.55A leads into **Lamp Office Court**. As early as 1702, this was a local base of the Conic Lighting Company, one of two firms then contracted to light the streets in the more affluent parts of London, and whose whale-oil lamps, though dismal by modern standards, were the envy of visiting foreigners. Flourishing here in the early 20th century was a Shaftesbury Memorial Hall. Today, housed in an old photographic studio, are the offices of the PR company Cube, whose showrooms are entered through **No.47**. This is one of a number of Grade-II-Listed 18th-century houses to have survived. Cross over and look back along the west side to take in the pleasing variety of shop fronts, serving an ever-changing succession of tradesmen.

Note the Doric pilasters at **No.51**.

Turn left along **RUGBY STREET**, which dates from c.1700, and was known until 1936 as Chapel Street. Note the row of wooden posts along the pavement of the north side. We first reach narrow 2-storey **No.20**, in dark red brick, which was (as No.19) the entrance to the Church of Humanity, alias Positivist School, opened in 1870 by Richard Congreve, Frederic Harrison and fellow disciples of the French philosopher Auguste Comte. Ritualistic 'services' took place in a room to the rear, where people of all social classes met in praise of humanity, encircled by busts of the great and the good of human history. The 'Religion of Humanity' had its own calendar of 13 months, with feast days honouring secular 'saints' from Socrates to Shelley, from Ptolemy to Priestley, from Romulus to Rossini. Dwindling support led to closure of the 'church' c.1932, and its premises soon became a dance hall. The building now houses a graphics and design company whose hanging board displays a mock coat of arms with the motto "By Appointment to the Royal Authority of Creativity".

No.18 next door is Victorian, but boasts a Georgian doorcase. Here in 1956, on 16 June – Joyce's Bloomsday – poets Sylvia Plath and Ted Hughes spent their wedding night in a flat belonging to one of Hughes' friends. They had married, with Plath's mother as the sole witness, at St George the Martyr. As Sylvia recorded (poignantly, in view of her later suicide): "We came together in that church of chimney sweeps with nothing but love and hope and our own selves." *18 Rugby Street* is the title of a poem in Hughes' *Birthday Letters* (1998).

Early-18th-century **Nos.10-16**, with white-painted porches boasting hoods on carved brackets, were further beneficiaries of Camden Council renovation. **Rugby Chambers** (1867), at No.2 beyond, was built on the site of the Episcopal Chapel of St John, which had given the street its original name, and was shown as "The Chapell" on a map of 1702. Although it was never consecrated, its pulpit attracted several eminent Anglican preachers, and William Wilberforce was numbered among its congregation. From 1827 the resident minister was the Rev. Baptist Wriothesley Noel, a fervent evangelical. In 1848 he abandoned the Chapel, which was demolished, and two years later lived up to his forename by converting to the Baptist faith, serving for 18 years as minister at nearby John Street.

Cross over to the **Rugby Tavern** on the opposite corner, created in the mid-19th century by knocking together two houses of the early 18th. Return along the south side of the street, past the Corinthian-pilastered shop at **No.7** that was once another pub, the King's Arms. Burrowing *through* one side of it is a very narrow 18th-century passageway, leading to Emerald Street (p 20) and known as **Emerald Court**, as

an official sign confirms. **No.13** beyond was previously the popular French's Dairy, whose attractive tiled shop front and fascia and name have been preserved by the costume jewellery designers who now occupy the building. The dairy was run by a succession of Welsh dairymen, including from 1870 John Jones, John William Davies and the Davies family until 1994. There is an old plaque stating that "In the rear is the White Conduit (circa 1300 AD), originally part of the water supply to the Greyfriars' monastery, Newgate Street". Identified a century ago, the conduit head still exists behind the shop. Edwardian antiquarians concluded that the lead-piped conduit predated 1258, and that the spring here was one of two feeding it, the other being north of what became Queen Square (p 27). This White Conduit should not be confused with a later, better-known namesake that ran from Islington to Charterhouse. The conduit here was decommissioned in 1727 and rediscovered only in 1907.

Regain **LAMB'S CONDUIT STREET**, cross over and turn left. Longstanding occupants at **No.45** are the undertakers A(lbert) France & Son, a family firm claiming a 400-year pedigree. The present proprietors are descended from "Mr France" of Pall Mall, who as "upholder to the King" organised the state funeral of Lord Nelson, prompting one wag to remark that "France got Nelson in the end". A tiny model of the admiral's magnificent coffin is on display

in the window. **No.35**, whose entrance is adorned with little lions' heads, was selling motor accessories in 1906, but had previously been a Home for Working Boys in London, and was later the base of the Gaelic League of London. Modern **Rapier House**, opposite, covers the site of No.40, where the Bloomsbury Synagogue stood for many years until the 1960s. The café on the next corner at **No.29**, inscribed "1887", was successively a chandler's, a dairy, a boot repairer's and a florist's.

Turn right along Dombey Street (p 20), and right again into **ORDE HALL STREET**. Dating from 1882, this was built on land acquired cheaply for slum clearance by the Metropolitan Board of Works, of which one John Orde Hall was a member. It supplanted the notorious Little Ormond Yard, originally Ormond Place. Although this had been described as a "dangerous and disreputable haunt of Irish beggars and thieves", contemporary census returns suggest that this was both a racist slur and a gross exaggeration. A night school for the education of the local poor, established in the yard in 1848 by the Working Men's College, would have had to compete with the pleasures of the Coach & Horses pub, opened some 5 years later. Built in yellow stock brick, the new street was once perfectly symmetrical, with terraces of modest houses on either side with decorative keystones over the doorways, and more substantial houses at each corner.

Of the latter, three survive, at **No.2** and at **No.29** and **No.30** at the north end, as does the eastern terrace, restored by Camden Council in 1976. The terrace on the west side was demolished after WWII. There today stand the council flats of **Babington Court** and 14-storey **Chancellor's Court**.

Beyond a children's play area, turn left along a footpath through the site of erstwhile (Great) Ormond Yard **[10]**, originally Ormond Mews. Here William Morris once rented space; as did an ageing William Brockedon (p 27), listed here as a manufacturer of "Cumberland lead" (graphite); an improved treatment for black lead had been among his numerous inventions. At Nos.23&24 was the forbiddingly named Mendicity Mill, where the Mendicity Society (p 16) provided 'mill work' for the destitute. By 1950 the yard had become a "mouldering slum" begging for demolition. Latterly a wilderness of tarmac and grass, it has now been refurbished.

Turn right into **BARBON CLOSE** (a modern naming after Nicholas Barbon, the rapacious late 17th-century speculator). The Victorian building on the right, now occupied by electrical engineers, was until the 1920s a mission hall and working

men's club of St George the Martyr church, witness the inscription "1876" and (beneath the chimneystack) the monogram "St GM". Emerge at the north end through a square-cut aperture, past a grubby signboard advertising "George Bailey & Sons, horse and motor contractors". A larger-than-life character, Bailey served as Mayor of Holborn in 1942-43. His multi-faceted

business flourished in Ormond Yard until after WWII. Perhaps the most exotic occupant of his stables there was an elephant from the circus-cum-zoo at Gamages, the Holborn department store.

A left turn along Great Ormond Street leads back to Queen Square, whence you may retrace your earlier steps northward to Russell Square station.

10   A late-17th-century house in erstwhile Ormond Yard, thought to have been the last galleried dwelling-house in London (photographed before WWII)

Route 4
Largely the Doughty estate

Sinuous walk from Holborn station to the Yorkshire Grey
(see back cover for map)

From Holborn Underground station, walk east along High Holborn. Crossing to the north side at the first set of lights, continue eastward. Beyond Red Lion Street, pass the front of MidCity Place, at No.79 High Holborn, whose other elevations we viewed in Route 1. Pass Hand Court (see *Streets of Old Holborn*) and take the next turning on the left, along narrow **BROWNLOW STREET**. Bordering Gray's Inn, this was built by William Brownlow (d.1675) on land in the manor of Portpool owned by his family since the 16th century. His daughter Elizabeth married into the Doughty family, who in time became landlords of the estate that is the subject of this walk. In 1826 the family became extinct and the land passed to their relatives the Tichbornes.

An 18th-century cast-iron pump stands where Brownlow Street meets L-shaped Bedford Row. It bears two heraldic shields, representing the United Parishes of St Andrew and St George the Martyr. Look left to see Georgian Nos.46-48 on the south side of what was originally named Warwick Place. Then walk a few paces east to glance along **JOCKEY'S FIELDS**,

the old mews area for the east side of the Row. The mews and its parent street were built c.1716-20 on a 3-acre plot known as the Jockey Field. Bebbington suggests that this could have been where horses were prepared for an annual ceremonial ride by the Lord Mayor and Aldermen of the City of London to inspect the City Conduit (off Oxford Street). The 1901 Census may be the last that shows almost all male heads of household in Jockey's Fields to have horse-related occupations: grooms, cab drivers, or keepers. Much of the charm of this street has been lost, the replacement of cobbled roadway with insensitive tarmac and yellow lines adding to the gloom of the Gray's Inn perimeter wall.

Now turn westward, then north, into broad, tree-lined **BEDFORD ROW** – named, of course, not after the Dukes of Bedford but after the charity whose estate we explored in Route 1, and on whose eastern boundary it lies. The first houses were erected by Nicholas Barbon from c.1690. The Jacobite sympathiser Mary Shireburne, later Mary Howard, Duchess of Norfolk, was born in the embryonic street in 1692. Its east side and south end lay on Brownlow-Doughty land, and were mostly developed by the Doughty family in the early 18th century. The Row was described in 1734 as "one of the most noble streets that London has to boast of". Elizabeth Cromwell, daughter of Oliver, died here aged 82 in 1731. At the

Crown Coffee House, which flourished in Bedford Row (c.1724-44), the rules of whist were first drawn up. Other early Bedford Row residents included Sir John Holt, Lord Chief Justice, who died here 1710; Sir William Garrow, Baron of the Exchequer; and William Warburton, Bishop of Gloucester and friend to both William Stukeley and Alexander Pope.

On the west side, which fared badly during WWII, many of the buildings are replacements in a fairly sympathetic neo-Georgian style. The east side, which is largely intact (but required some post-war reconstruction), presents many fine doorways, with early Georgian horizontal hoods and elegant fanlights. Especially fine is **No.11**: you may be lucky enough to glimpse its first-floor interior wall and ceiling paintings by John Vanderbilt, which were probably executed after 1720, for Dame Rebecca Moyer. The paintings include an equestrian George I, and allegorical figures of the Arts and Britannia. A later resident, after 1776, was landlord Henry Doughty. The British Printing Industries Federation moved into the house in 1938, later absorbing adjacent war-damaged **No.10**. Born in 1757, probably at the latter address, was Henry Addington, who as the 1st Viscount Sidmouth **[11]** was the uncompromising Home Secretary at the time of the Peterloo massacre (1819). *The Bedford Row Conspiracy* was a humorous story by Thackeray, published

11 Henry Addington, 1st Viscount Sidmouth, born 1757 in Bedford Row

in 1840. Lawyers by then shared Bedford Row with institutions of various kinds: the Entomological Society, founded in 1833 at **No.12**, the Lord's Day of Rest Association at **No.13**, and the Ironmongers' Association at No.48. John Abernethy, the eccentric surgeon who founded the medical school at Bart's hospital (c.1781), lived at **No.14**, which later became offices of the Masonic Union.

Among the well-established craftsmen who lived and practised their trade in Bedford Row were John Mills, a cabinet-maker and upholsterer (in 1790-1809), and Charles Parman, carver and gilder (in 1790-93). However, the profession that had so resented Dr Barbon's intrusion into the area (p 14) had been quick to colonise the resulting streets, and to this day the Row remains largely a preserve of solicitors and barristers. Among these was the law reformer and promoter of art Edwin Wilkins Field, whose office was at No.41: in the 1840s, he campaigned to reform solicitors' remuneration and the arcane Court of Chancery; he called for a single location for the Royal Courts of Justice, and as their secretary was involved in acquiring "the Carey Street site".

Continue to the far corner, and Edwardian **Bank Chambers** at No.24. The "ULB" monogram above the door recalls their former occupation by the Union of London Bank, later merged into the National Provincial.

Cross Theobalds Road at the pedestrian lights, and proceed down the east side of **GREAT JAMES STREET**, Bedford Row's narrower, treeless continuation, where solicitors' offices abound. Among the best preserved of local streets and another feast of hoods and fanlights, though on a more intimate scale, it was built from c.1721 by George Brownlow Doughty and his wife Frances, in association with one James Burgess (from whom the street name is derived).

There are many literary connections in Great James Street. The poet Algernon Charles Swinburne spent two periods at **No.3** in the 1870s. When his friend Watts-Dunton (see below) first called with a letter of introduction, he surprised a naked Swinburne who chased him onto the pavement, but nevertheless befriended the poet and set about rescuing him from his life of debauchery. Frank Swinnerton, critic and writer of London-set novels, lived at **No.4**. E V Lucas, who edited Charles Lamb and wrote for *Punch*, was at **No.5** in the 1890s. From 1923-30 Leonard Woolf worked at **No.38** (opposite) as literary editor of *The Nation*.

At **No.6** is a splendid Neo-Classical mahogany porch, graced by a frieze of delicately carved festooned urns. Gerald Brenan, the novelist and Hispanophile, lived at **No.14** in 1927-29, in what he described as "the most beautiful street in London". He contrasted the glory of the fine panelled staircases with his small attic flat and its "18th-century fireplace full of mousetraps". Two doors beyond, at **No.16**, Brenan's friend David Garnett, the author of *Pocahontas* (1933), was a partner in the Nonesuch Press run by Francis and Vera Meynell. **No.15**, in between, was home in 1872-73 to Theodore Watts-Dunton, friend of Swinburne (see above) and himself a minor poet, also solicitor to Dante Gabriel Rossetti, and a camp-follower of the Pre-Raphaelites. The house today is the headquarters of the Federation of Master Builders.

Across the road at **No.28**, and celebrating the achievements of women, is the Sybil Campbell Library, here since 1998. Sybil Campbell (1889-1977) was a barrister and the first woman stipendiary magistrate, who founded the library in 1928, at Crosby Hall, Chelsea. It includes donations from eminent scholars of the interwar period: Bertrand Russell, Beatrice and Sydney Webb, and Virginia and Leonard Woolf. The novelist George Meredith lived in the 1840s at his father's house, **No.26**. The architect John Shaw jun. (1803-70) was born at **No.25**: he was surveyor to the Eton Estate in Belsize in the 1840s, where he is thought to have designed Eton Villas. Some houses at the north end of the street have been re-fronted. **Nos.23-24**, rebuilt in the 1960s, incorporate what Cherry and Pevsner describe as an "inept" re-use of a very

grand doorcase with phoenix adornment, brought from long-since demolished 30 Great Ormond Street (p 34). As a blue plaque suggests, the detective-story writer Dorothy L Sayers settled at No.24 in 1921, staying for over 20 years.

Turning right into Northington Street (Little James Street until 1936), we pass the end of **COCKPIT YARD**, on the site of a fashionable 18th-century cockfighting venue, described in 1816 as the only remaining London cockpit still "having any vogue". A Victorian musical instrument warehouse has in turn given way to upholstery and framing, and sausage and shrimp-paste factories in the early 1900s, to what are now **Cockpit Arts** promoting the work of many artist-designers here and across the UK, and the **Cockpit Workshops** of Camden Council. In **NORTHINGTON STREET** itself, old houses remain at **Nos.17-21**, but **Nos.18&20** opposite are a recent pastiche. Robert Henley, Earl of Northington, was Lord Chancellor in the 1760s. No.16, now flats, was a 20th-century rebuild of a public house known for two centuries as the White Lion. In the late 1980s it was renamed the Dickens, hence the preserved portrait of the novelist on the corner. The paved area signed **KIRK STREET,** named after John Kirk (p 49) is all that remains of former Robert Street, late Victorian tenements which ran north to join Roger Street before WWII. In 1901 it contained over 100 households,

whose residents followed diverse occupations: bookbinders and printers, a perfumer's assistant and a food preserver.

A little way into **JOHN'S MEWS** on your right a white concrete building was Holborn Assembly Hall; during WWII this was the local Civil Defence headquarters. Holborn Library, whose back entrance is at the far end of this cul-de-sac, was itself built on what had been a Civil Defence training ground. In the northern (left) part of John's Mews, beyond the red-brick **School House**, the western side is taken up with the latest (1970s) incarnation of **St George the Martyr C of E Primary School**, here on its fourth site, and now separated from its mother parish. Until 1904, the northernmost end of the Mews was called John's Place.

Continue east along **NORTHINGTON STREET**, past **No.13**, a low Dutch-gabled building bearing stone plaques dated 1903, and erected by members of the Finch family. At first a coach builders', it later became a garage, and was converted to flats in 1997. Opposite stands a curious building, partially tiled and with a row of canted bay windows supported on outsize brackets. It is mainly 2-storey but rises to four, presumably to match the height of adjacent No.28 John Street. Although once numbered (as No.12), it was never separately listed in any ratebook, and seems to have been simply a late-Victorian side extension, built in the garden of its

Georgian neighbour. Messrs Shrigley & Hunt, a firm of glass painters here in 1904, would doubtless have appreciated the generous natural light offered by the large windows.

At the junction with John Street is the **King's Arms**, retaining a typical 19th-century wooden pub front. Its sign is bizarre, featuring the arms of the Tudor monarchs (with fleurs-de-lys in place of the Irish harp), supported by a predictable lion and an unexpected fox. Continue eastward as Northington Street drops gently towards the Fleet valley. Two old wooden shopfronts are worth a second glance: at **No.8**, with its slightly bowed window, and at **No.11**, the pre-WWII home of tennis-racket makers, Leslie Coates. We are entering a one-time industrial enclave, west of Gray's Inn Road, where the workshops that colonised the local mews were joined by several small purpose-built factories. On the left stood the Victorian concertina works of Lachenal & Co., later superseded the present-day **No.4**, an imposing Art Deco building with blue metal windows, and now offices for design companies. It began as the Premier Works of Robert Rigby Ltd, "scientific engineers". Beyond, at **No.2**, the premises of Jacob's, plumbers' merchants, were closed for renovation in 2008. Surgical truss makers were still operating here in 1942. A major customer, no doubt, and with offices in nearby Great James Street, was the Rupture Society,

whose main objective was the "gratuitous provision of trusses". With its ground-floor windows barred against thieves, **No.3** (opposite, and originally No.1) was devoted first to scientific instrument making, an occupation much associated with the Italian community, and occupied later by Brown & Englefield, manufacturers of pewter goods for confectioners and ice-cream makers.

Intersecting from the south is **KING'S MEWS**, once a stabling area for residents of King's (now Theobalds) Road. Turn, however, along **NORTH MEWS**, its northward continuation, whose east side housed for many years the sanitary-ware factory and showroom of S Jacob & Son. Crossing Roger Street, continue ahead along **BROWNLOW MEWS** (cf. Brownlow Street, p 43). Modern brick-built flats line the east side, facing old mews buildings opposite. Remnants of hoists survive at **No.27A**, long occupied by wheelwright Charles Courtney; and at **Nos.24-26**, now photographic studios, but for decades home to the shopfitters Sims & Woods. The same firm occupied **No.22**, while rival shopfitters J H Bridgman had workshops behind. Note the fine glazed first-floor taking-in doors and large windows. The premises now house the London Dramatic Academy of Fordham University, New York, whose patron is Dame Diana Rigg. **No.21** was home from c.1897 to Moule's Patent Earth Closet Co.

Retracing your steps, turn left into

ROGER STREET. Here (c.1900) were a printers' ink works serving the staple industry of the locality, and a joinery works. The offices at **No.12** cover the site of the late-Victorian chocolate factory of Dr Tibble's Vi-Cocoa Co. Ltd. Imagine the heady mix of aromas which must have permeated these streets from both that and the nearby Reid's brewery in Clerkenwell Road! Roger Street was originally named Henry Street after Henry Doughty, an association lost when it was arbitrarily renamed in 1937. The slightly winding street follows the line of the much-mentioned Fleet river tributary, forming part of the boundary between Holborn and St Pancras parishes, and their successor boroughs. Again crossing John Street, we pass on the right an oval wall-mounted boundary plate, dated 1821. Continue ahead, passing the **Duke (of York)** pub, rebuilt in the 1930s on its original site at the foot of John's Mews (p 45), in which stand the adjoining contemporary flats of **Mytre Court**.

Turn right into **DOUGHTY MEWS**, a tastefully renovated backwater put to a mixture of residential and commercial uses. On the left corner, the triangular shape of **No.29** is the result of the old parish boundary which followed the line of a tributary of the River Fleet. The (now disused) Post Office Mail Rail tunnel also runs beneath, a further problem for the architects' practice of Cany Ash and

Robert Sakula when executing its first commission. From 1980 until his death in 1992, **No.4** was home to the Argentine-born recluse Ricardo Caminos and his private Egyptology library. Next door at **No.3** are the offices of the Egypt Exploration Society. **No.20**, farther along on the left, appears to have preserved three original double-leaved stable doors.

At the far end, turn right along Guilford Street, staying on the south side, and pausing where **DOUGHTY STREET** crosses. Despite its overall uniform appearance, this wide street was built gradually over 30 years, beginning in 1792, when its development by Henry Doughty (as Upper John Street) was prompted by the Foundling estate's eastern extension of Guilford Street over Doughty land (p 51). Notice the variety of styles in the railings, balconies and fanlights. To your left is a short section of Doughty Street running to the north of Guilford Street into Mecklenburgh Square. Nos.20-28 on the west side were destroyed in WWII, and replaced by part of London House (p 54). Gothic revivalist architect William Butterfield lived in 1848-54 at No.24, in a street popular with architects. Though **Nos.32-38** opposite survived the war and are original, their neighbours at **Nos.29-31** are faithful reconstructions. William Ruff, author of *Guide to the Turf*, lived in 1844 at the original No.30, which was later the birthplace and home in early life

of poet Charlotte Mew (1869-1928); her father Frederick was another architect. The portrait painter William Lawson was living at former No.29 with his wife and family from 1860 to 1867. The building served in 1891 as Fellowship House, headquarters of the Fellowship of the New Life, an early socialist experiment in communal living, whose joint secretaries at that time were Edith Lees (the future bride of Havelock Ellis, who lived there) and Ramsay MacDonald, then newly arrived in London. *From Doughty Street to Downing Street* is the title of Herbert Tracey's 1924 biography of the first Labour prime minister.

Turn southward along the west side of Doughty Street, where **No.19** had a critical role in WWI. It was from here that carrier pigeons were despatched to the front in France. The Germans disliked the pigeon service, and tried to bomb Doughty Street several times: but mercifully no birds or men were lost when a bomb fell in an adjacent garden. When the service expanded, **Nos.17-18** were requisitioned. In the interwar period, No.19 continued as the office of 'Racing Pigeon' Publishing. The publisher and bookseller William Tegg, a friend of Dickens, lived at **No.15**, though this was not until 1852-95. "Correspondences are like small-clothes before the invention of suspenders; it is impossible to keep them up". Such was the wit of the Rev. Sydney Smith (1771-1845) who, as a plaque

12   The witty Rev. Sydney Smith
(undated portrait by Henry Perronet Briggs)

ROUTE **4**

records, lived at **No.14** in 1803-6. When the "wittiest man in England" lectured at the Royal Institution, the "concourse of carriages" gridlocked parts of Mayfair. His sermons were serious. As a freelance clergyman, Smith **[12]** preached at chapels in Mayfair and Fitzrovia, and in the evenings at the Foundling Hospital (p 54). No.14 was later home to James Agate, the film and drama critic.

The journalist Edmund Yates, who lived almost opposite at **No.43** for six years in the late 1850s, described the street as "none of your common thoroughfares to be rattled through by vulgar cabs and earth-shaking Pickford vans, but a self-including property with a gate at each end, and a lodge with a porter in a gold-laced hat, with the Doughty arms on the buttons of his coat", preventing those not on business from "intruding on the exclusive territory". (Baroness) Dr Edith Summerskill, a later Labour politician, was born at **No.46** in 1901; as an MP (1938-61) and life peer, she campaigned on health issues and women's matrimonial rights. **No.48** was, in 1837-39, the first marital home of Charles Dickens, shared not only with wife Kate and son Charles, but also brother Fred and sister-in-law Mary Hogarth who, after a trip to the theatre, expired here in the novelist's arms. Here he wrote most of *Nicholas Nickleby*, and all of *Oliver Twist*. The name of Mr Brownlow, Oliver's elderly benevolent friend, was possibly inspired by that of Brownlow Mews at the rear of No.48. The house was acquired in 1924 by the Dickens Fellowship and transformed into the treasure-house of Dickensiana that is Dickens House, now known as the Charles Dickens Museum.

In later life, the builder Thomas Cubitt lived farther along at **No.53**, from 1837 until 1849. The following year, J M Levy, founder of the *Daily Telegraph*, moved into **No.57**. The reformers and feminist authors Winifred Holtby and Vera Brittain (mother of Shirley Williams) lived in Doughty Street in 1922-23 after leaving Oxford, initially at **No.52**; a blue plaque erected in 1995 at **No.58** identifies the second flat they shared. Earlier and present at the 1861 Census with his young family was publisher Frederick Warne, who at that time was working with brother-in-law and fellow publisher-bookseller George Routledge. **No.62** today serves as offices of the Fulbright Commission, created by US Senator J William Fulbright in the aftermath of WWII to promote peace and understanding through educational exchange.

Continue ahead along **JOHN STREET**, named after the carpenter to the Doughty family, John Blagrave. It is one of the area's gems, with splendid doorways and a glorious variety of architectural detail, though 20th-century intrusions slightly mar the overall effect. The upper west side had been built by 1760, but the rest of the street was completed only some 40 years later. By the latter part of the 19th century, its fine 'first rate' houses, built for affluent Georgian families, had been converted into offices for charities and trade associations; for solicitors, accountants, quantity surveyors, and the occasional publisher.

On the west corner with Roger Street, at **No.21**, the offices of **Haines House** date from 1938, sporting the easily missed figures of two female nudes atop the bulky stone entrance. The large **Bedford House** (No.21A) next door, built after WWII in inappropriate plain red brick, and now occupied by solicitors, stands on the site of John Street Baptist Chapel. This opened in 1818 and flourished here until ravaged by enemy action in WWII. The houses beyond at **Nos.22-25** are notable for their rectangular fanlights.

They face an eastern stretch which contains notable examples of 18th-century architecture. The houses have arched doorways with imposing outsize doors surmounted by semicircular fanlights, and railings with urned finials. The Open Air Mission founded in 1853 is still at **No.19**. At **No.15** is the Chartered Institution of Water & Environmental Management, whose centenary in 1995 is celebrated by a plaque. A large (working) clock hangs outside **No.11**, still inscribed "Royal Oak" after the benefit society of that name, based here until the early 1980s. **No.10** housed Holborn's first public library, opened in 1891, and served as a welfare centre during WWII.

South of the King's Arms, the east side of the street is a mixture of original and rebuilt houses, where porticoes with broken

13   Holborn Central Library: official opening, 22 Nov 1960: H M the Queen Mother inspects the art exhibition on the 3rd floor

pediments predominate. Until the 1950s the Africa Inland Mission occupied **No.3**. 20th-century **No.1** is a former branch of the Westminster Bank, now converted into flats.

Meanwhile, on the west side, **No.30** was home, in 1847-58, to the Ladies' Charity School, founded in St Sepulchre's in 1702, with royal patronage, and later removed to Queen Square (p 29). **Nos.31-32**, rebuilt in facsimile, were headquarters from 1914 of the Shaftesbury Society & Ragged School Union. A bust and plaque honour John Kirk, "Christian philanthropist and friend of children", and a mainstay of the charity for many years. After its departure for SW1 c.1960, the Metropolitan Water Board (later Thames Water) moved in, appropriately in view of the district's water supply associations; a newspaper group is now in occupation. **Nos.34-36**, with especially fine Ionic porticoes, date from 1760, while **No.33** is a modern reconstruction. The Law Commission overlooks Gray's Inn gardens from **Conquest House**, a 1950s red-brick block.

Arriving again at **THEOBALDS ROAD**, turn to the right to arrive at **Nos.32-38**. This is **Holborn Library [13]**, opened by the Queen Mother in 1960 as a central library for the former Metropolitan Borough, and much acclaimed at the time. Cherry and Pevsner praise Borough Architect Sidney Cook's creation of a lively street front with its pattern of hexagonal

ROUTE **4**

49

concrete panels below the two floors of continuous glazing and brick-faced top storey. The visitor who takes the stairs to the library's upper floors will find the least altered part of the building: attractive wood and grey/white mosaic-patterned panelling, and windows offering tantalising views towards the former Midland Grand Hotel's pinnacles at St Pancras International. The library has undergone many changes, including the opening here in 1995 of the Camden Local Studies & Archives Centre, whose excellent resources (documentary and human) have been indispensable to the authors of this book and its sister volumes. From its windows, the varied architecture of Jockey's Fields (p 43), across the road and to the right, may be best appreciated.

From the library entrance, continue briefly west to note two new arrivals in March 2008: a small café-cum-cakeshop of the kind existing in this street until WWII, and described by Winifred Holtby in *Letters to a Friend*; and opposite, at **Nos.5-11**, the Royal College of Paediatrics and Child Health.

Retracing your steps, cross John Street, and pass at **Nos.12-22** a short but imposing Georgian terrace (c.1770), with fine doorways, and railings topped by torch flambé finials. These houses survived the 1878 road widening, for unlike Theobalds Row to the west, this end of the King's Road had been spared the earlier depredations of Barbon

and his contemporaries, had remained of a generous width, and scarcely needed widening. At **No.22**, a plaque commemorates the birth here, in 1804, of the future prime minister Benjamin Disraeli. The house, then No.6 King's Road, was the home (1802-17) of his father Isaac D'Israeli, a man of letters whose routine included a daily stroll to the British Museum.

The smart Corinthian doorway at present-day **No.6** beyond once gave access to a teashop of the ubiquitous J Lyons chain. The jazz saxophonist and leader of Pieces of Eight, Harry Gold, was a longtime resident of Theobalds Road from 1942 until his death in 2005, living at **No.8**, Dartmouth Chambers. Next door, at the junction with Gray's Inn Road, is the **Yorkshire Grey** pub (rebuilt 1877), its equine name perhaps influenced by the cavalry barracks that once stood in Gray's Inn Road (p 78). Over the main door is a gilded horse's head, while high above in the gable is a colourful effigy of a mounted cavalryman. This is best seen from the opposite corner, where stands the former Holborn police station of 1896, still inscribed "Police" but taken over in recent years as offices for Gray's Inn.

Turn south along the lower reaches of Gray's Inn Road to reach Chancery Lane Underground station or make use of one of the several local bus routes.

Route 5
Around Coram's Fields
Circular walk from Russell Square station
(see back cover for map)

Captain Thomas Coram, a shipwright and master mariner born in Lyme Regis, settled in Rotherhithe in about 1720 after nearly 30 years in New England. Appalled by the regular sight of infants abandoned to die in London streets by their hapless mothers, he campaigned for 17 years for the establishment of an institution to protect them. Twenty-one "Ladies of Nobility and Distinction" were eventually persuaded to petition George II, and the Foundling Hospital (FH) was established by Royal Charter in 1739, opening in cramped accommodation in Hatton Garden. Two years later Coram's "ladies", and some gentlemen, bought from the 6th Earl of Salisbury a 56-acre field called Conditeschotte north of Lamb's Conduit. Because the Earl refused to sell less than the whole of the field, the FH had land surplus to requirements. The 'hospital' (really a form of orphanage) was built near the middle of the property, on the site of present Coram's Fields, leaving undeveloped meadow land on either side and to the north.

In 1756 the FH received a parliamentary grant, but this was withdrawn four years later, leaving the institution in a parlous financial state, and by 1790 it was forced to consider developing its spare land for housing. Though keen to raise income, the governors were anxious to preserve "the advantages of its present open situation" **[14]** for their young charges, and to ensure a development that would "rather raise than depress the Character of this Hospital itself as an Object of National Munificence". Leafy Brunswick and Mecklenburgh Squares, flanking the FH site and each with houses on only three sides, reflect this aspiration. Plots were let to a number of speculative builders, pre-eminent among them the young Scot,

James Burton, who was also active on the Duke of Bedford's estate to the west. By 1802 he had built 586 houses on the Foundling estate. The architect Samuel Pepys Cockerell was appointed as surveyor.

This walk covers the eastern half of the Foundling estate, although we start in the west. Turn left on leaving Russell Square station, then left again along Herbrand Street to reach **GUILFORD STREET**. Lord North, Duke of Guil(d)ford, was president of the FH. Cross over to its south side, which is now almost wholly modern. At the corner with Russell Square is the 8-storey **President Hotel**, on the site of

Bolton House, successively home in the 18th century to Lord Baltimore, the Duke of Bolton, and Lord Loughborough. The adjacent pathway leading into Queen Square was known before WWII as Bolton Mews. Walking east, observe the terrace of Georgian houses opposite at **Nos.61-81**, some with original façades. Laid out in 1792, Guilford Street was built mainly by Burton in the following five years, many houses having chimneypots made at nearby

14 'When the Foundling Hospital stood on salubrious site'; reproduced from a curiously captioned print published in 1751

Bagnigge Wells (p 75). Notice the off-white band running between ground and first floors of some houses. Cockerell planned the street to comprise 'first-rate' houses at the west end, reducing progressively to 'fourth-rate' further east. The 'stone string' was to run continuously along the whole length of the street to disguise the gradual degradation in quality, an effect wholly lost in 20th-century redevelopment.

The Celtic Hotel at **No.62** was bought in the early 1930s by Evan Evans, a Welsh-speaking dairyman turned car dealer and hotelier, and the founder of what became one of Britain's largest private coach-tour operators. Evans also served as a wartime Conservative mayor of St Pancras. The journalist and novelist George A Sala **[15]** (see also p 58) lived at **No.64** in 1864-6. **No.67** was home (1801-17) to the botanist and physician John Sims, FRS, a foundation fellow of the Linnean Society, commemorated in the Mexican genus of compositae named Simsia. The house was later home (1834-50) to the engineer John Farey, whose *Treatise on the Steam Engine* had been published in 1827. Four people died in a disastrous fire here in 1844, two of them policemen. Two future Lords Chancellor were neighbours: Sir Thomas Wild (later Lord Truro), at **No.69** (1814-44), and Sir Edward Burtonshaw Sugden

(Baron St Leonards), at **No.71** (1822-44). Doric-pilastered **Nos.70-73** were rebuilt after wartime bomb damage, and of **No.74** only the ground floor remains. Here, in 1801-19, lived the Lord Chief Baron of the Exchequer, James Scarlett, later Baron Abinger. **No.77** was briefly home to Sydney Smith, the divine and wit, on first arriving in London in 1803 and before moving to Doughty Street (p 47).

On the south side, meanwhile, between two pedestrian entrances to Queen Square (p 27), the flats of **Guilford Court** and **Queen Court** occupy the site of No.54, home in 1852-61 to architect Matthew Digby Wyatt (p 63).

Opposite, beyond Grenville Street, the Guilford Arms pub was a further victim of the Blitz. The rear of International Hall (p 60) now covers the entrance to former Guilford Mews, and the site of No.81, where the antiquary William Durrant Cooper died in 1875. A sometime solicitor to St Pancras Vestry, he gave evidence in 1833 to a House of Commons committee on the negligent way in which incumbents were keeping parish registers. Behind sealed doors at surviving **Nos.89-92** is student accommodation now absorbed into the adjoining hall of residence.

Lining the south side of Guilford Street, and adorned by a frieze depicting the nine Muses, is the **Princess Royal Nurses' Home**, designed for the nearby children's hospital by Stanley Hall, and improbable

15   'Journalism': G A Sala caricatured in *Vanity Fair*, 25 Sep 1875

winner of the RIBA London Medal in 1936. Church architect William M Teulon lived on the site at No.42 in 1854-67. Beyond, the 1960s block of the world-renowned (Nuffield) **Institute of Child Health** covers the sites of the University's post-WWII Model Welfare Clinic, of former Lansdowne Mews, and of No.33. The latter was home to medical journalist Thomas Henry Wakley, editor of *The Lancet* and son of its founder; and here was born in 1851 his own son Thomas, the journal's third editor. The poet Swinburne (also p 44) lived in 1879-80 at No.25, which later became the Edwardian West Central College of Music, Art & Languages. Demolished No.24 was immortalised by Thackeray in his *Ballad of Eliza Davis*:

In this street there lived a housemaid,
If you particklarly ask me where--
Vy, it vas at four-and-twenty
Guilford Street, by Brunsvick Square.

The 'decadent' poet Ernest C Dowson, a friend of Yeats, later lived round the corner in **GUILFORD PLACE**, the northern egress from Lamb's Conduit Street, which was once named Lamb's Conduit Place. Cockerell had a crescent in mind when he planned the Place, as the shape of the roadway suggests, but builders balked at the cost of building it, and William Harrison, who undertook the task in 1793, substituted a square-cut shape, as evidenced by the old houses remaining

at **Nos.3-6** on the east side. Here in the 18th century stood the Coach & Horses tavern, where on dark winter evenings in 1756 an armed escort could be hired by pedestrians wishing to walk north through the dangerous fields to the Bull at Kentish Town. The central traffic island contains a long-closed underground lavatory, not Victorian as might be imagined, but installed by St Pancras Council in 1931. Here too is the long-disused Francis (*sic*) Whiting Fountain, donated in 1870 by the Misses Whiting in memory of their mother, and adorned by a statue sculpted by Henry Darbishire (designer of Peabody dwellings and of the Baroness Burdett-Coutts fountain in Victoria Park). Depicting the Woman of Samaria pouring water from a jug, it clearly alludes to neighbouring Lamb's Conduit. Guilford Street was built on the banks of the Fleet tributary which fed the conduit, and the New River Company was initially unwilling to lay on a water supply to the street, claiming that the ground was too soft for its pipes.

Across **GUILFORD STREET Coram's Fields**, on the site of the Foundling Hospital, which was closed in 1926, as central London was no longer considered a healthy environment for children. Most of the buildings were demolished, and the land was sold, the proceeds being used to build a large boarding school at Berkhamsted. Today we can only imagine the grand buildings (see front cover)

that once stood in the middle distance, beyond the striking green-roofed 20th-century 'pavilion' (shelter). Designed by Theodore Jacobsen, a founding governor of the FH, the buildings opened in 1745. In the centre was the chapel (p 59), which soon became a highly fashionable place to worship, the novel institution having excited much interest and curiosity among the upper classes. East and west wings housed respectively girls and boys: the sexes were always segregated, except on Christmas Day.

Around the edges of Coram's Fields are the few FH buildings to escape demolition in 1926. On the far left, the Mary Ward Boys' Club moved into **No.93**, currently being renovated. At the entrance are two lodges and between them a vacant plinth, on which stood a statue of Thomas Coram (by W Calder Marshall, 1852), now removed to Berkhamsted. In a niche in the plinth is a wordy copper plaque, with a short history of the site. Cross over, if you will, to inspect it. In an earlier niche hereabouts, desperate mothers once left their babies in a basket, before ringing a bell and departing. They came from all over the country to seek admission for their offspring, and the hospital was unable to cope. FH admission policies varied greatly over time. For a while there was a balloting system, whereby the acceptance or rejection of an infant was determined by the drawing of a white or a black ball. Infant foundlings were farmed out to an army of foster parents all over England until the age of four, when they returned to the FH until their early teens. The regime was spartan, but remarkably humane by the standards of the day. Children were always treated as individuals, each receiving a name, often of a FH governor or his wife, or of a character from history or literature. Girls, on leaving, usually entered domestic service, while boys became apprentices or joined the armed services. The FH aimed to give them an education befitting their lowly status in life. Of the two colonnades surviving on either side of the playground, that on the west side was at one time used by the boys for making rope, which was sold for use by the fishing fleet. Since 1977 it has housed a flourishing miniature city farm with sheep, goats and chickens.

When the FH closed, most of its land was sold to a property speculator named James White, whose plan was to relocate Covent Garden market onto the Hospital site, and to transform nearby streets into an industrial estate, a proposal mercifully despatched by a huge local outcry. A fund-raising campaign to turn the site into a children's playground reached its target with generous help from newspaper magnate Harold Harmsworth (Lord Rothermere). Opened in 1936 as the Harmsworth Memorial Playground, and claiming with justification to be "the world's finest", it now serves local children from numerous cultural backgrounds. Please note the unusual, but prudent, rule that adults are admitted only if accompanied by a child!

Continue along the south side of Guilford Street, past London University's 1960s computer centre. It covers the site of the house at No.23 into which the sculptor Jacob Epstein moved with his wife Margaret in 1916. Campaigning unsuccessfully to be appointed a war artist, he was conscripted the next year as an ordinary private. Beyond Millman Street stood No.13, where in 1919, as newly-weds, the poet Edwin Muir and novelist Willa Anderson set up home in two ground-floor rooms. Willa was then working in "a cramming institution in Red Lion Square", presumably the University Tutorial College (p 16).

Past Doughty Mews (p 46), some late-18th-century houses survive, with Cockerell's white stone string again in evidence. By Edwardian times, most had become boarding houses, small hotels, or offices. **No.10** was then the headquarters of the Rational Dress League, a group advocating practical clothing for (especially) women. A plaque records the opening here in 1990, by Sarah, Duchess of York, of a Sick Children's Trust "home from home", for parents of patients at nearby Great Ormond Street Hospital. Alongside, **No.11** houses the Kurdish Human Rights Project, founded in London in 1992; and **No.8** is now the headquarters of NADFAS (the National Association of Decorative & Fine Arts Societies).

Beyond Doughty Street another plaque, at **No.6** (now the Guilford Hotel), recalls an earlier St Nicholas's Nursery, also connected with GOSH. Born in 1900 at **No.2** was Henry Sherek, the theatre manager, who in his time presented or produced over 110 plays in London, including several T S Eliot premières. By 1916 the house was shared by a Salvation Army 'slum settlement' and Moule's Earth Closet Co.

Cross again to the north side, and return westward. Samuel Birch, who died in 1841 at **No.107**, had a finger in many pies – as a poet and playwright, as a colonel in the militia and as Lord Mayor of London. A great character of his day, he was satirised in a skit as the 'emperor of London'.

Re-crossing Doughty Street, reach the site of demolished No.102. Here was the practice of the architect Charles Reeves, designer of 64 Victorian county court buildings nationwide. George Shepheard, the watercolour painter and engraver, died of dropsy in 1842 at No.100, his home for 21 years. On the site today is **London House**, the original block of **Goodenough**

16 Mecklenburgh Square (p 56), south-east corner, sketched by Hanslip Fletcher in 1926, and showing its since demolished south side (right)

College. Now housing postgraduates of both sexes, it began as a hall of residence for male students from the Dominions. F C Goodenough, chairman of Barclays Bank, was the driving force behind its promoters, the Dominion Students' Hall Trust. The southern block here, its ground floor faced with knapped flint, was designed by Sir Herbert Baker and opened by Queen Mary in 1937. A stone plaque on the south wall records the dedication of the house library to engineer Sir Charles Parsons (1854-1931), who perfected the compound steam turbine.

Pass the gated entrance to the College and take the next turning right into short **MECKLENBURGH PLACE**, known until 1938 as Caroline Place. On the Ordnance Survey map of 1936, it appeared disarmingly as Sally Place, a name presumably proposed but rejected because, with its topical Gracie Fields connections, it was considered too plebeian for its princely surroundings. It had by then become a colony of doctors' surgeries.

We are soon in quiet and peaceful **MECKLENBURGH SQUARE**, possibly our area's best-kept secret (**[16]**, p 55). The square got its name from George III's wife, Queen Charlotte, who was the daughter of the Grand Duke of Mecklenburgh-Strelitz. Actress Flora Robson lived in 1936-37 at No.6 in the south-east corner, where war-torn houses gave way to an extension of previously three-sided London House, built by the London Goodenough Trust in 1961 to form a quadrangle, with an entrance here in Mecklenburgh Square.

The houses and private gardens of the square (c.1810) were designed by Joseph Kay, a pupil of Cockerell, who had by then resigned his surveyorship in a huff, having been accused of failing to enforce standards: not all the builders active on the estate were as scrupulous as Burton. Cockerell now magnanimously supervised Kay's work here as an unpaid consultant.

The east side of the square, fronted by a generously wide roadway, was based loosely on Robert Adam's work in Fitzroy Square, its magnificent façade intended to attract the right kind of resident to this less favourable end of 'Bloomsbury'. It is only partially stuccoed – fine rendered sections, adorned with wreaths and festoons, alternating with plain brick – probably for effect rather than economy. Nos.21-25, the stuccoed centrepiece, bear four Ionic columns. So pleased were the FH governors that they paid Kay eight times the fee he had requested. In the 1930s the London Welsh Association was at **No.11**, backing onto what is now the London Welsh Centre in Gray's Inn Road (p 80). The Welsh language was often to be heard in a pub on the corner of nearby Millman Street called the Portland Arms (after the Duke of Portland, FH President in 1793). So, at least, reported Graham Greene, who in 1938 rented a studio in the square where, high on benzedrine, he worked on *The Confidential Agent* every morning and *The Power and the Glory* in the afternoon.

At **Nos.12&13** were the post-WWII offices of the Nuffield Foundation. Francis Wormald, the palaeographer and art historian, lived until 1941 with his wife in a flat at **No.14**. Living with his in-laws, at **No.15** from 1855, was the portrait painter James Hayllar, whose wife Ellen was an aunt of nurse Edith Cavell. Their thirteen years here saw the birth of nine children, every one of whom became a professional painter. **No.18** was home to the illustrator Marjorie Quennell, and later (1932-35) to the poet laureate John Masefield.

In an area where blue plaques are rare, **No.21** boasts two – to R H Tawney, the socialist historian, who lived here with his wife in later life (after many years at No.44, p 58); and to Sir Syed Ahmed Khan, the Muslim reformer and scholar, resident here in 1869-70, who after working in the Indian Civil Service had come to England to secure a Western education for his two sons. Helena Normanton, the lawyer and feminist campaigner, lived with her husband between the wars at **No.22**. The first female barrister to *practise* in England, she campaigned for divorce reform and equal rights for spouses, and was the first married British woman to be issued a passport in her maiden name. Earlier, in rooms specially rented in the square, Catherine Pine, the nurse and suffragette, cared for the four female 'war babies' adopted by Emmeline Pankhurst in 1915. **No.23** is now a Goodenough College residence and club. From 1858 to 1915 the West Central Collegiate School, one of the longest surviving dame schools (see also p 37), was at **No.25**, later to become the base of the Baptist Women's League. Nos.22-25 were a post-WWII residence of the ENT hospital (p 88) in Gray's Inn Road.

Nos.29-34 served as an interwar nurses' home for the Royal Free Hospital, also in Gray's Inn Road. The flats of war-damaged Byron Court (Nos.26-34) were rebuilt as a fair facsimile, though now with a single entrance at **No.26**, and disappointingly modern dormer windows. Mary Braddon, Soho-born writer of 'penny dreadfuls' and later of such highly popular 'sensation fiction' novels as *Lady Audley's Secret* (1862), moved in 1861, with her mother, into the home at No.26 of her employer, the publisher John Maxwell, posing as his wife and acting as stepmother to his five children. (Maxwell's real wife was in a Dublin mental institution.) Living and working at the same address in 1868-97 was theatre architect Charles Phipps, who reconstructed the Theatre Royal (Haymarket) and went on to design the Savoy, the Lyceum and Her Majesty's. Tancred Borenius, the Finnish art historian and diplomat, settled at No.29 after his marriage in 1909 to his boyhood

sweetheart, Anne-Marie Runeberg, granddaughter of Finland's national poet. The chemist Samuel Parkes, whose *Chemical Catechism* went through 13 editions, died at No.30 in 1825.

Leading from the north-east corner of the square is short **MECKLENBURGH STREET**. No.11 on the war-ravaged west side was the birthplace in 1845 of Henry Sweet, the phonetician much admired by George Bernard Shaw and often said to have been the model for Henry Higgins in *Pygmalion*; Shaw did concede that "there are touches of Sweet in the play". Later, at the same house, and until her untimely death in 1928, the classical scholar Jane Harrison shared a lesbian relationship with her student, the poet Hope Mirrlees. On the east side the 4½-storey houses at **Nos.1-8**, with a continuous row of iron balconies, miraculously survived WWII. No.1 was a hotbed of anarchism c.1900, and during WWI the headquarters of the Anti-Conscription League.

HEATHCOTE STREET, beyond, was named after Michael Heathcote, a FH governor from 1810. The street was virtually flattened in wartime bombing, and **Nos.1-5** on the north side are a modern neo-Georgian pastiche. One survival was the old red-and-white street sign, on the south side to the right: "leading to ... Caroline Place", anachronistically declares. Set in the pavement nearby is a plate marking the Foundling estate

boundary. A bar gate here once protected the good folk of Mecklenburgh Square from unwelcome intrusions, but today the only gates are the ornate ones guarding the entrance to St George's Gardens (p 66) at the west end of the cul-de-sac. Bollards now prevent cars from entering the square from the north-east, and contribute substantially to its peaceful air.

Returning to **MECKLENBURGH SQUARE**, walk along its secluded north side, half of which is occupied by **William Goodenough House**. The female counterpart of London House, this was run by the 'Sister Trust' until it merged with the male establishment in 1965. An inscription records its erection 8 years earlier, aided by the Lord Mayor's National Thanksgiving Fund. On this site was No.35A, the 1930s home of actress Fay Compton. In 1939 the basement of No.37 became the headquarters of the Hogarth Press. Virginia and Leonard Woolf moved here that year to escape the noise of building work in Tavistock Square, only to be bombed out in 1940 while away at their country retreat at Rodmell, Sussex. The scene of devastation greeting them on their return is vividly described in Virginia's diary. Likewise demolished No.38 was home in 1906-11 to artists Sir William Nicholson and his better-known son Ben. Sampson Low, the publisher (also p 39), died at No.41 in 1886.

Surviving beyond is a fine terrace of 4½-

storey houses, with grand double doors and fanlights. Living in 1857-60 at **No.43** was Sir William Cubitt (1785–1861), the canal and railway engineer – no relation to the Cubitt building dynasty of Gray's Inn Road (p 72). **No.44** was home to a strange household in 1917. D H Lawrence wrote part of *Women in Love* while staying here with his wife Frieda as a guest of Dorothy Yorke. Dorothy's lover, writer Richard Aldington, was then away at the Front. His wife, Hilda Doolittle (the American imagist poet 'HD'), was meanwhile elsewhere in the house, recovering from a miscarriage. It is poetic justice, perhaps, that Hilda is the one commemorated by an unofficial blue plaque. After WWI, Dorothy L Sayers moved in, and here created Lord Peter Wimsey. Unhappy with the neighbourhood – where, she alleged, "drunks and wife-beatings [were] pretty common" – she moved on, investing the fruits of her success in No.24 Great James Street (p 44). The historian R H Tawney then moved with his wife into No.44, where they lived until after WWII. On the first day of the Somme offensive, Tawney had been critically wounded by machine-gun

fire, and rescued only after lying for hours in no-man's land. Destined to live with pain and discomfort for the rest of his life, he would pad around No.44 in his carpet slippers and old khaki sergeant's tunic. The same house was home in 1946 to Eric de Maré, the architectural photographer. Successive 1930s residents at **No.45** were theatre critic Harold Hobson and the publisher and author John Lehmann, who bought Virginia Woolf's share of the

Hogarth Press. Living at **No.46** in 1878-84 was the travel writer George A Sala (also p 52), whose neighbour at **No.47** was the eccentric widely travelled actor, writer and artist Lewis Strange Wingfield. This house later became the Foundling Hospital School of Domestic Economy.

On the left at the north-west corner of the square is the boxy brick **Wolfson Centre** of the Institute of Child Health, on the site of the earlier Coram's

17 Praps you know the Fondling Chapel,
   Vere the little children sings:
   (Lor! I likes to hear on Sundies
   Them there pooty little things!)
   The Ballad of Eliza Davis (Thackeray)

Fields Primary School. To the right is **Coram Community Campus**, once part of the FH garden, and known as Coram's Garden in more recent times. It was part of 2½ acres of land leased back when the rest of the FH site was sold. Here is the headquarters of Coram Family, known until recently as the Thomas Coram Foundation, which continues Coram's legacy in the provision of services to vulnerable children and for young people leaving care. Adoption, Child Contact, and Housing & Support Services are provided. Visible at the northern edge of the site are two FH buildings of the late 19th century – a small mortuary and an indoor swimming pool (with a clerestory roof). Outside the Campus gates, bear momentarily left and follow a permissive footpath westward. On your right is the Thomas Coram (Early Childhood) Centre, a successor to the St Leonard's Nursery School erected here in 1939.

The Coram's Fields football pitch on the left marks roughly the site of the main blocks of the Foundling Hospital. The central block housed the chapel where daily services were held for 'Thomas Coram's children', dressed in a characteristic uniform **[17]**, right up until WWI. Handel's donations included a copy of the score of his Messiah, and an organ for its chapel (now in St Andrew's, Holborn). Though sidelined by the governors, who considered him a nuisance, Thomas

Coram, on his death in 1751, was buried as he wished in a vault beneath the Chapel. Later removed to Berkhamsted, his remains are now in St Andrew's Church, Holborn. Charles Dickens had a pew in the gallery of the chapel, and Tattycoram in *Little Dorrit* was a 'Foundling'.

Emerge into the north side of **BRUNSWICK SQUARE**, named after Caroline of Brunswick, the wife of the Prince Regent. To our right is a statue of Coram (by William MacMillan, 1963) in front of No.40. Designed by J M Sheppard, the building was erected in 1937 to house the FH art collection and the Thomas Coram Foundation's HQ. A bust of the Captain surmounts the entrance, while the Court Room inside is an exact replica of that in the old FH, incorporating the original rococo plasterwork on walls and ceiling. The many paintings in the building include William Hogarth's satirical *March of the Guards to Finchley*, and his magnificent portrait of Coram, from which the statue outside is derived. Hogarth, a founding governor, persuaded many notable artists such as Reynolds and Gainsborough to donate their work to the FH, which became, in effect, London's first public art gallery. No.40 opened to the public in 1998 as the **Foundling Museum**. Also on display on the top floor there is the Gerald Coke collection of Handel memorabilia.

Brunswick Square was developed earlier

than its easterly neighbour; of the relatively plain (and eventually run-down) houses built here by Burton in 1795-1802, not one survives. Though never fashionable, the square was always respectable: Macaulay referred to "the quiet folk" who lived there. It is praised in Jane Austen's *Emma*, where the heroine's married sister Isabella proclaims that "our part of London is so very superior to most others ... we are so very airy". Dominating the north side today is the red-brick bulk of the University's **School of Pharmacy** (founded in 1842), designed by Herbert J Rowse and begun in 1938, but not fully occupied for over thirty years. At its official opening in 1960, the Queen Mother jokingly described it as the "oldest new building" in London. The painter Michael Wishart was born on the site in 1928 at No.39, the elder son of Ernest Wishart, the publisher. No.37 at this time was a YWCA hostel. Nos.32 and 34 were successively home in 1803-16 to John Hunter, a physician and FH vice-president who gave his name to nearby Hunter Street (p 67). No.32 was occupied in 1854-62 by the caricaturist John Leech (also pp 32, 62). Five 'Bloomsberries' lived at No.38 in 1911: Virginia and Adrian Stephen shared the house with John Maynard Keynes, Duncan Grant and Leonard Woolf until the following year, when Virginia and Leonard married and left.

Ahead, the west side of the square is now wholly lined by the modern cantilevered terraces of The Brunswick (p 71), and its imposing east 'portal'. On this side the novelist E M Forster, a friend of the Woolfs, lived in 1929-39, first at No.25 and then at No.26. Away from his mother's Surrey home, his London pied-à-terre gave him the opportunity to meet the male acquaintances with whom he had casual relationships.

In 1812-19 the lawyer and poet Bryan Waller Procter (p 14) worked in several solicitors' practices in London. William Maginn, the Irish poet and future editor of the scurrilous literary journal known as *Fraser's Magazine,* moved with his wife into lodgings here in 1824. At No.28 was the Minerva Club, founded in 1920 by Elizabeth Knight, doctor and campaigner for women's suffrage. The residential club, open to "men and women in sympathy with progressive thought", attracted many former militant suffragettes, and became the headquarters of the Women's Freedom League.

Make your way to the south-east corner of the square across recently renovated **Brunswick Square Gardens**. Near their centre is Camden's finest example of a London Plane tree. On the square's south side, Nos.4-5 housed the Home for Women Artists in London, the first of its kind and founded in 1879 by Baroness Burdett-Coutts and Louisa Twining (p 31). Raphael Meldola, the Jewish chemist, who discovered the first oxazine dyestuff, known as Meldola's blue,

died suddenly at No.6 in 1915. On the south side today is **International Hall** (1962), a London University student hostel, whose ground-floor walls are enlivened by the badges of 21 (sometime) Commonwealth countries, with the curious addition of Austria.

Eastward lies short **LANSDOWNE TERRACE**, built c.1792 as Lansdowne Place, after the eponymous Marquis who was Prime Minister at the time. On the left are a part of the FH's western colonnade (p 54), and a strip of grass where city-farm sheep sometimes safely graze. Surviving opposite are Burton's **Nos.1-4**, recently refurbished and incorporated into International Hall. From 1939-49, part of Selwyn House at No.2 was the HQ of *Horizon,* the avant-garde arts magazine launched by Cyril Connolly and edited by the poet Stephen Spender. The flat it occupied was to have been the marital home of Spender and his first wife Inez, had she not suddenly left him. During WWII, contributor George Orwell often slept in the offices at No.2, despite the noise from the anti-aircraft battery in the nearby square. (He would eventually marry Sonia Brownell, the magazine's Girl Friday.)

Backtrack along Brunswick Square's south side to the roundabout, and turn left into **GRENVILLE STREET**. The street took its name from Lord Grenville, Foreign Secretary in 1791-1801. On its

west side are the flats of **Downing Court**, and the Café Romano at **No.11**, which was the Foundling estate office until the 1970s. **Nos.8-10** were only recently rebuilt – Georgian pastiche – on what had remained a bombsite for half a century after the end of WWII; the lost houses had previously been a nurses' home of the ENT hospital in Gray's Inn Road (p 88).

An archway, surmounted by a carved inscription, leads into cobbled **COLONNADE**, along which we turn, and which was long known as Colonnade Mews. Determined to preserve the district's residential character, the FH governors allowed commercial development only in this south-west corner of the estate. The south side long consisted of stables, once a preserve of horse-cab proprietors and now predictably serving as garages and workshops. They once faced onto a colonnaded shopping parade. Above one shop were assembly rooms, where Dr Roget (p 72) sometimes lectured. By the 1870s the small Georgian shops had become a slum, and were demolished to provide back gardens for the residents of Bernard Street. Some of these have recently been sacrificed to 2-storey pale-brick flats, with curious copper roofs, named **Chandler**, **Baker** and **Tailor Houses** in memory of trades that flourished here two centuries ago. Halfway along on the left, a Victorian taking-in door and gantry survive at **Nos.19-23**. Nearer the ground (and sometimes obscured by parked cars) are reminders of the boundary of St Pancras with St George's Bloomsbury: the parts of the Foundling estate within the latter parish are covered in the next walk (Route 6). At **Nos.29&31**, now 'Perfect Pictures' (film and video post-production specialists), Evan Evans (p 52) first opened his Woburn Garages and started dealing in cars.

At the west end of the Colonnade is the **'Horse Hospital'**, 2-storey stables for 24 horses, dating from 1797, attributed to James Burton and Grade-II-Listed. Original features preserved include tethering rings, ramps whereby horses reached the upper level, and an original floor with troughs for their urine to run away. Since 1992 the building has housed the large Contemporary Wardrobe (costume) Collection, an art gallery (the Chamber of Pop Culture) and KinoCulture, a cinema club showing cult and underground films.

Turn right, past the old **Friend at Hand**, a public house originating in Georgian times, into **HERBRAND STREET**, here once narrower and accessed at each end by covered entries, and numbered as part of the Colonnade. Disregard the supposed potted history of the pub on display outside: despite its title it describes a wholly unrelated establishment, the Globe on Marylebone Road! Turn right again to return to your starting point at Russell Square station; or proceed, maybe, to Route 6.

Route 6
East and west of Marchmont Street
Circular walk from Russell Square station
(see back cover for map)

Most of the area covered by this walk lay in the parish of St George's Bloomsbury, and thus in the later borough of Holborn. Almost all was built up on the estate of the Foundling Hospital, and several of the street names recall FH benefactors.

Leaving Russell Square station, cross the road (Bernard Street) safely, bear left and turn right along **HERBRAND STREET**, which forms the eastern boundary of the Bedford estate. This first section was formerly Little Guilford Street but was re-named in 1901 when Herbrand Arthur Russell, 11th Duke of Bedford, was also the first Mayor of Holborn. By then it had deteriorated into something of a slum. Off the east side lay Bernard Mews, and by 1881 the National School of Christ Church, Woburn Square. On the opposite side today, on the site of old Woburn Mews East, is the eccentrically-shaped Art Deco building, in cream-painted stuccoed concrete, designed in 1931 by Wallis, Gilbert & Partners, architects of the Hoover factory. It was originally a multi-storey garage for the

Daimler Hire Co., its own cars occupying the upper level with public garaging and a waiting-room beneath. Later becoming the depot and coach station of Frames Tours (p 64), and more recently the London Taxi Centre, the Grade-II-Listed building now serves as offices of the long-established advertising agency McCann-Erickson.

Pause on the corner by the colossal modern concrete 'chimney', thought to be connected with the local water supply. Here **CORAM STREET** intersects. Dating from 1800-04, and originally named Great Coram Street, it once continued eastwards to Brunswick Square across the site of The Brunswick (away to your right). The street's present-day rump is entirely 20th-century. Diagonally opposite to your left, 1930s **Witley Court** flats, with their prominent fire escape stairs, occupy the site of the Russell Institution ([18], p 62). Erected speculatively by James Burton in 1802 as assembly rooms, it burned down the next year and was rebuilt as a literary and scientific club, founded, with fellow lawyers, by the judge James Scarlett (later Lord Abinger); the Duke of Gloucester was its first president. Thackeray and Leech were members, as was Charles Dickens. With a library eventually holding 16,000 books, the Institution flourished for most of the 19th century.

The **Holiday Inn** is fronted by a colonnade of lamp holders. The hotel was previously a Forte Posthouse and

18 The Russell Institution,
Coram Street in the 19th century.
Witley Court (1930s) now covers the site

earlier still the Bloomsbury Crest Hotel, built by McAlpines back-to-back with the firm's HQ (p 72). On the hotel site, former No.9 was home in 1860-62 of early feminist publisher Emily Faithfull. Here she founded the Victoria Press, where female compositors were controversially employed. Queen Victoria, not usually sympathetic to feminist ideas, appointed Emily "printer in ordinary to Her Majesty". At adjacent No.13, in 1837-43, lived William Makepeace Thackeray, then

struggling to establish himself as a writer. His wife Isabella had a mental breakdown when their third child was born, and had to be entrusted to a Paris sanatorium. In his *Vanity Fair*, Mr Todd lives in Great Coram Street. Thackeray shared the house in 1837 with the caricaturist John Leech (p 36), and 5 years later with Edward Fitzgerald, the translator of Omar Khayyam's *Rubaiyat*.

Continue north along **HERBRAND STREET**, here once named Little Coram Street, and accessed through a narrow

archway at the north end. The west side is occupied today by **Coram**, **Thackeray**, and **Dickens Houses**, three red-brick blocks of municipal housing separated by lawns, erected by Holborn Borough Council on land bought from the Duke of Bedford in 1898, and replacing the mean courts of Abbey Place and Tavistock Mews. The municipal blocks contrast with the earlier **Peabody Buildings** opposite, eight blocks in stock brick built around a courtyard in 1884, after slum clearance by the Metropolitan Board of Works expunged Coram, Russell, Marchmont and Chapel Places. Financed through the generosity of the American George Peabody, who bequeathed £½ million to rehouse London's "respectable poor", they are still administered by the Peabody Trust. The estate is recognisably the model for Brown's Buildings, home of the heroine in *Marcella*, the 1894 novel by Russell Square resident Mrs Humphry Ward [19].

Pass the diminutive Bloomsbury Ambulance Station at **No.19**. This was one of the first six ambulance stations built by the LCC when the London Ambulance Service was established in 1915. Reach **TAVISTOCK PLACE** and turn left. The western extremity of Tavistock Place lay on the Bedford estate, hence the name, 'Marquess of Tavistock' being the title of the heirs to the Bedford dukedom. The rest of the road was on the Foundling estate. It was radically renumbered in

1938 after merging with Compton Street, its easterly extension. On the south side, Tavistock Mansions at **No.16** occupy the site of a house at No.9 that was home in 1810-11 to James Elmes, the architect, antiquary, and compiler of *Metropolitan Improvements*. **Nos.2-14**, a mid-1970s neo-Georgian pastiche, replaced houses begun here in c.1805 by James Burton. Successive residents at No.10 (then No.2) were the antiquarian John Britton in 1811-20, and slavery abolitionist Zachary Macaulay (p 34) in 1835-37.

Once standing opposite at No.37 was a large villa occupied 1826-44 by the stockbroker and astronomer Francis Baily. Here he conducted experiments to "weigh the earth" or, more accurately, to determine its density. A detached house, set back from the road, was essential to avoid interference from vibrations. It was later occupied by Matthew Digby Wyatt, the architect responsible for the decorative work at Paddington Station.

Eastward today stands the **Mary Ward Conference Centre**. In 1890 Mrs (Humphry) Ward opened a social centre at University Hall in Gordon Square, followed a year later by clubs for men and boys at Marchmont Hall, which survives behind Nos.82&84 Marchmont Street. Newspaper owner John Passmore Edwards was persuaded to finance a new building in Tavistock Place for a 'Settlement', to provide ordinary people with educational

19   Mary (Mrs Humphry) Ward (1851-1920)

and social amenities normally available only to the rich. An architectural competition judged by Norman Shaw was won by two University Hall residents, A Dunbar Smith and Cecil Brewer. Their creation, opened in 1897 as the Passmore Edwards Settlement,

with a library and large hall, has been hailed as a triumph of Arts & Craft design. Preserved within are rooms occupied by the Settlement's early middle-class residents and, in the basement, a double-height gymnasium. Within a year Mrs Ward had opened Britain's first play centre there, and the first school for disabled children. She died in 1920, and a year later the centre was renamed, after her, the Mary Ward Settlement. Under this name it housed the Tavistock Little Theatre, which later became a wartime refuge for Italia Conti's bombed-out stage school (p 20). In 1961 the freehold was bought by the Nuffield Trust, and the building was restored for occupation by the National Institute for Social Work, becoming variously known as Mary Ward Hall and Mary Ward House.

Beyond an old school gate **No.9** was built in 1906 to house Mrs Ward's aforementioned school. As an LCC School for the Physically Defective, and later as the Mary Ward Primary School, it continued to offer special education until 1961. When the Nuffield Trust took over Nos.5-7, the boys' club migrated to Coram's Fields, while other Settlement activities moved into No.9, renamed the Mary Ward Centre, pending a permanent move to Queen Square (p 28). The building is now home to the Camden Chinese Community Centre.

Continue east. Ahead on the right is a continuous range of early houses at

ROUTE **6**

Nos.18-44, many of them now small hotels. In May 2008 the French street artist 'JR' pasted an enormous paper mural onto the side wall of No.18. Exactly 100 years earlier, Lenin took a flat at **No.36** (then No.21) while on a visit to London to study at the British Museum. On the north side, by contrast, nothing original remains. **No.11** covers the site of No.34, once home to Mrs Mary Ann Clark, a mistress of the ('grand old') Duke of York, second son of George III. At first a hotel, No.11 (with No.13) was an interwar and WWII headquarters of RAF Coastal Command. **No.13** later housed a substation of St Pancras Borough Council's municipal electricity service. Former No.33, on the site, was where Jerome K Jerome 'chummed' in 1889 with George Wingrave, the model for George in *Three Men in a Boat*.

A small gap marks the site of No.32, home in 1815-23 to the Scottish novelist John Galt. From 1853, it housed an English Kindergarten. The kindergarten movement had been founded in Germany by Friedrich Froebel, its objective "to help a child's mind grow naturally and spontaneously". In 1851 all German kindergartens had been closed down by a Prussian government fearful that they would nurture a generation of radicals. Moving from Hamburg, Bertha and Johannes Ronge established their second 'infants garden' at No.32, together with an 'Association school' for older children. The kindergarten thrived, and Charles Dickens was a frequent visitor. Later run by the two Praetorius sisters, it was taken over in 1879 by the Froebel Society, which set up here a short-lived Kindergarten [Teacher] Training College. Penelope Lawrence, the principal until its closure in 1883, went on to become headmistress of Roedean.

East of No.32, from 1803, stood the proprietary Tavistock or Woburn Chapel, a neo-Gothic blend of brick and stucco [20] described as "one of the first pretended revivals in this town of our Ancient Architecture". Beneath it were vaults for 1,000 burials; an episcopal Sunday school for 1,733 boys and girls opened behind in 1837. Its extremely High Church practices often landed it in trouble with the bishop. In 1882 it became an official District church, known as St Andrew's, Tavistock Square, whose minister was a curate of St Pancras. By 1892 the Anglicans had abandoned the chapel, which soon became a "Salvation Catholic Church and training hostel". Charles Booth reported in 1898 that "St Andrew's Temple" had "lately closed because the salvationist running it was defraying his expenses by ordering bicycles and then pawning them". Subsequently a cycling school and cabinet factory, it was demolished in 1900. Now on the site, **Nos.15-17** were designed as the headquarters of Express Dairies, probably by Charles Fitzroy Doll, architect of the Russell Hotel. More recently the HQ of British Transport Police, the building has now been acquired to serve as an annexe of the London School of Hygiene & Tropical Medicine.

Marchmont Street now intersects. Continue ahead along the eastern end of Tavistock Place, named Cox Street at first, and then Compton Street until its merger with the western half in 1938. According to a plan of 1801, before house building began, the street had a differently aligned precursor: a roadway labelled "The Parade" is shown running diagonally south-east from the crossroads, offering residents of northern Bloomsbury easy access to their parochial burying ground (see below). If it ever materialised, the route must have been short-lived, as by 1814 the development of Compton Street, on its present alignment, was complete. On the north side today, through a gap between Nos.21&23 Tavistock Place, the remains of Marchmont (Mission) Hall can be seen. Beyond is the baroque-style red-brick **Nos.25-31**, Egmont House, which were the post-WWII headquarters of the major travel agents, Frames Tours. It is now the HQ of the University and College Union, formed in 2006 and the largest trade union and professional association for people working

20 The Tavistock or Woburn Chapel, later St Andrew's District Church, demolished 1900 (from an undated *Prospectus*)

in further and higher education. On this site, at No.48 (later No.27), were the pre-war offices of the Crusade of Rescue and Homes for Destitute Catholic Children.

A covered entry leads underneath a stuccoed original house that was a pub in the 19th century into sunken, still cobbled, **COMPTON PLACE**. Samuel Compton Cox, of Bedford Row, was the FH treasurer in 1806. In Victorian times it housed a receiving station, police station, mission hall and ragged school. Today it is the entrance to the privately-run youth hostel known as The Generator (p 93), incorporating on the north side former McNaghten House, originally a police section house and from 1992 a hostel for the homeless.

Walk on along **TAVISTOCK PLACE**, past the mansion flats **Knollys House** (left) and **Seymour House** (right), each erected by the London Housing Society (LHS, see p 92). Cross Judd Street. The Builder's Arms pub which once stood on the northeast corner of this crossroads was among the casualties of a V2 rocket attack on nearby Regent Square in February 1945.

Continue east to where **WAKEFIELD STREET** intersects. Underlying Compton Street (see earlier) was a narrow field acquired by the FH when it developed its estate, but previously owned by Charles Fitzroy, Lord Southampton. It is not known whether Wakefield Street took its name from the nearby Pindar of Wakefield

pub in Gray's Inn Road (p 105) or from Wakefield Lodge, the Fitzroy family's Northamptonshire seat. To your left, off the north end of Wakefield Street, there once lay Wakefield Mews. Off its east side today are the council flats of **Selsey** and **Stanstead**, each bearing a Sussex place-name (see p 108).

Turn right, however, into the southern half of the street. On the right, **No.1** houses the Reta Lila Weston Institute of Neurological Studies, founded in 1977 with the aim of furthering knowledge about stroke and neurodegenerative disorders. It is part of UCL. Farther along on that side at former No.13 a pair of young transvestites, Ernest Boulton (b.1848?) and Frederick Park, took rooms in the late 1860s. Here they kept an extensive wardrobe of female attire and ornaments. As 'Stella' and 'Fanny', the coquettish duo appeared in music halls and theatres to rapturous applause, as well as frequenting restaurants and shopping arcades. Arrested in 1870, absolved of sodomy by illegally conducted medical examinations, and tried for "conspiracy to commit a felony", they were surprisingly acquitted, partly on grounds of their youth. On the site now is the UCL Department of Human Communication Science.

The church-like red-brick building opposite at **No.7** was the lecture hall of the original Scotch Church (p 108), which it adjoined. It is now the London

Ikeda Peace Centre of the Soka Gakkai International, a Buddhist association with more than 12 million members worldwide. Beyond, in what was once Regent Square Mews (and later Regent Buildings), is a former dairyman's yard, used in the 19th century by the milk contractors Freeth & Pocock, and more recently home to a bottling plant of Express Dairies. Facing west stood the Henrietta Street Chapel, a Baptist establishment that flourished here from 1822 to 1909. It later became the Regent's Working Men's Club, and was known before WWII as the Regent Square Institute.

Gates lead into the delightful green oasis that is **St George's Gardens**, and was once two burial grounds. You may care to rest on one of the benches on the left. In 1715 the Church acquired two parallel plots here on the very edge of town to serve as cemeteries for the future parishes of St George the Martyr and St George's Bloomsbury, which respectively occupied the plot's southern and northern halves. The grounds were laid out by Nicholas Hawksmoor. A brick wall constructed in 1806 separated the two sections, half of it surviving on your right today. In 1855 the by then badly overcrowded burial grounds were closed. With St Pancras Vestry support, the northern part was laid out as public gardens in 1884-85 by the Kyrle Society, a forerunner of the National Trust founded by Octavia Hill's sister Miranda, "for bringing beauty home to the people"; disused graveyards were to be transformed into "sitting rooms for the poor". Opened by Princess Louise (then Marchioness of Lorne), the gardens were extended five years later, taking in half of the southern section. The rector of St George the Martyr would not part with the other half, which he had lucratively leased in 1877 to Thomas Cooke, FRCS, the proprietor of London's last private school of anatomy. His dissecting room was in a "tin shed" behind the wall on your right. The land was granted in 1935 by the rector of St George the Martyr, in return for an annual pension of £100, to Mayfair estate agent John Cyril Lees Collingham. On his death a year later he, in turn, left the ground to the FH trustees "for the welfare of children for all time". Later known as Collingham Gardens, the ground is now occupied by the parent-run Collingham Gardens Nursery, not visible from here.

Wander through the gardens, past the drinking fountain (donated by Mrs Orbell), and bear right. Notice the selection of old gravestones along the boundary walls, and how fragments of tombstones laid in the grass mark out the line of the (here demolished) 1806 dividing wall. The obelisk on your right was erected in 1729 by Thomas Falconer. Farther on, also on the right, is the chest tomb of Anna Gibson, the sixth and favourite daughter of Lord Protector, Richard Cromwell.

Near the far south-east corner, and topped by an urn, is the grave of Robert Nelson. Relations of deceased parishioners were at first reluctant for them to be buried here in such an out-of-the-way spot, until Nelson, a leading lay churchman of his day, opted to be interred here and others followed suit. For a while the graveyard was known as Nelson's Burial Ground. Others laid to rest here were William Brockedon (p 27) and Zachary Macaulay (p 34), and in 1767 Nancy Dawson, the famous hornpipe dancer at Drury Lane. Also interred here were the headless bodies of twelve Jacobites, hanged, drawn and quartered in 1746. Here occurred a very early recorded case of grave-robbing: in 1777 two resurrectionists, one of them a gravedigger, were sentenced to six months' imprisonment, and a whipping at the cart's tail from Kingsgate Street to Seven Dials, a traditional route for such spectacles. Follow a more northerly path back to where you entered the gardens. The terracotta statue of Euterpe, muse of lyric song, was salvaged from the façade of the demolished Apollo & the Muses pub in Tottenham Court Road, and donated in 1961 by Anthony Heal. Beside the exit is the tiny Mortuary Chapel of 1806, known today as the Chapel of Ease, and used for meetings of the Friends of St George's Gardens, through whose encouragement the overgrown open space was restored by Camden Council

with a lottery grant, reopening in 2001.

Outside, to the left, is a short (once L-shaped) cul-de-sac named **HENRIETTA MEWS**. Past 'The Cottage', an erstwhile gardener's residence, it leads to Collingham Gardens Nursery. By the entrance to the Mews the kerbstones are inscribed "SPL" and "SGB" recording the north-eastern extremity of the oddly shaped parish of St George's Bloomsbury. At this point **HANDEL STREET** joins Wakefield Street at a right angle. It was originally called Henrietta Street – after the wife of Sir Stephen Gaselee (d.1838), a FH vice-president – but was renamed in 1887 after the famous composer, a benefactor of the FH. 4½-storey Georgian houses, partly refaced, remain on the left-hand side at **Nos.4-7**, sandwiched between two small mansion-flat blocks, **Handel** and **Brunswick Mansions**. George Russell French, genealogist and architect, who died at No.6 in 1881, had in 1835 unsuccessfully submitted a Tudor Gothic design for the new Houses of Parliament. The **Bloomsbury Surgery** opposite covers the site of the Brunswick Pavilion (**[21]**, p 68) a fine 2-storey house and garden advertised for sale in 1810 as a suitable residence for a nobleman.

Handel Street is bisected by busy **HUNTER STREET**, built on the line of an old track running north from Lamb's Conduit and named after Dr John Hunter, physician and FH vice-president who lived in Brunswick Square (p 59) – and *not*, as often supposed, after his contemporary namesake, the royal surgeon and anatomist whose collection can be seen at the Hunterian Museum in Lincoln's Inn Fields. Pause at the junction to observe the opposite side. No.54, at its south end, was the birthplace of author and art critic, John Ruskin. As a small boy he loved watching water-carts being filled from a stand-pipe outside, through "beautiful little trap doors and pipes like boa-constrictors". The

Drawn & Engravd by J.Wallis, 159.Fleet Street.

house, which had borne a commemorative plaque, was swept away to make way for the Brunswick Centre (see later). So too was No.48, the Victorian home of the Society for the Employment of Necessitous Gentlewomen, which offered them tuition and employment in the arts of printing, engraving and bookbinding. To your right, on the site of **Hunter House** (another LHS property), John Sell Cotman, the famous watercolourist, lived at No.42. He was here for eight years (while drawing master at King's College) until his death in 1842, after which his less famous watercolourist son, Miles Edmund Cotman, moved in. Adjoining to the north are **Grenville Mansions** and **Cambria House**, a Salvation Army hostel now run as a residential training centre.

Cross Hunter Street by the pedestrian crossing and look back to the east side. Here, to your right, two early houses survive, at **Nos.3&4**. The journalist William Weir, Dickens' successor as editor of the *Daily News*, died in 1858 at No.4. Nearby, it is said, was the sometime residence of Mrs Maria Anne Fitzherbert, the Catholic widow married secretly and illegally to the Prince of Wales (later George IV) in December 1785. The house stood north of Handel Street. On its site today is the former Royal Free Hospital Medical School for Women, a pioneering establishment opened in 1874 by Mrs Elizabeth Garrett Anderson, which survived here as a medical

school for over a century. It was designed in a 'Queen Anne domestic' style by John McKean Brydon, of whom Elizabeth's sister Agnes was an architectural pupil. Restored by Avanti in 1988, it now serves as the **Hunter Street Health Centre**, with the Bloomsbury Surgery behind. The building has an imposing portico with a broken pediment. Many of its details are imitated in **Jenner House** (c.1913), the London Housing Society mansion block to the north, named after Edward Jenner, the smallpox vaccination pioneer. No.13, on the site, was home from 1857 to Ellen Ranyard, who here founded the Biblewoman Movement, formally known as the London Bible and Domestic Female Mission, an eventually international body that survived till the mid-20th century. Ellen's aim was to supply London's poor with Bibles and this, she believed, would be best accomplished not by city missionaries, but by working-class women; Marina, her first assistant, was recruited from the slums of St Giles. The mission later ran a dormitory for watercress sellers and established a district nursing scheme. Ellen's son, the astronomer John Cowper Ranyard, died at No.13 in 1894.

Continue along the western half of **HANDEL STREET**, passing on the left the sites of the pre-WWII Greyhound pub and of the Barham Works of the Co-operative Printing Press. Here today are the management offices of The Brunswick

and an imposing glass entrance to Waitrose supermarket. Beyond, and extending through to Marchmont Street, are the diminutive, private **Marchmont Gardens**. On your right is the **Territorial Army Centre**, alias Yeomanry House, also the base of the University's Officer Training Corps. It was built c.1908 as the drill hall of the 1st (City of London Battalion), the London Regiment, previously based in Fitzroy Square and earlier still in Queen Square. On the site, at long-demolished No.19, Ugo Foscolo, the Italian patriot, died in extreme poverty in 1827. The building rounds the corner, as shall we, into the rump of **KENTON STREET**. Benjamin Kenton, a tavern waiter turned vintner, made a fortune by inventing a means of bottling ale so that it could be shipped to seamen in hot climates without the cork popping out. He left his money to charity, the FH being among the beneficiaries. His eponymous street once continued south, across The Brunswick site, where it had subsumed early Wilmot Street (John Wilmot was an FH vice-president in 1791-1810), off the east side of which lay Brunswick Mews, later renamed Calsen Yard. Kenton Street would no longer exist at all if, as originally planned, the Brunswick Centre (left) had been continued northwards to Tavistock Place.

Turn right along Kenton Street's surviving end, where No.20 on the west side once housed the organist and composer Joseph Kemp. From 1810 he lectured on musical education at the Russell Institution, advocating (maybe for the first time in England) the teaching of music in classes and the playing of exercises by pupils in concert. Refurbished **Aberdeen Mansions** and **Robsart Mansions** are all that remain of a row of six mansion flat blocks, c.1900, mostly named after works of Sir Walter Scott (*Ivanhoe, Kenilworth*). Comic magician Tommy Cooper lived in Waverley House in 1952-55. The Victorian survival at **Nos.73-75** was long a printer's, but the preserved metal sign here recalls post-WWII occupants, the builders & contractors C & E Norris. Note the taking-in door and hoist.

Briefly retrace your earlier steps west along Tavistock Place to the traffic lights at **MARCHMONT STREET**. Pause here. Originating in the early 1790s, the street was named after Hugh Hume (1708-94), Earl of Marchmont and a FH governor. At first largely middle-class residential, it developed into a typical Victorian local 'high street'. In 1877-78 Marchmont Street was renumbered and substantially rebuilt. Virginia Woolf (*Diary*, 5 April 1924) loved the street, describing it as "like Paris". Some shops thrived here for generations. The fishmonger's business of Samuel Gordon on the north-east corner of the crossing with Tavistock Place closed in 1997 after 120 years of trading. Balfour's,

a long-established bakery at **No.77** on the south-west corner, was an earlier casualty of rising costs and diminishing custom, and is now an Italian restaurant of the same name. The bakery's Victorian fascia and red-and-green tilework were lovingly re-created by the restaurant's new owner in 2007. The prominent inscription "est.1826" on the north-west corner of this crossing probably relates to the business of Thomas Willis, a tea merchant who opened a branch here in the 1890s.

On the west side to the north of the crossroads, No.26 (on the site of the former Express Dairies shop at **No.87**) was where Percy Bysshe Shelley, wife Mary, and stepsister-in-law Claire Clairmont stayed in 1816 before visiting Byron in Geneva. An archway, still labelled "South Crescent Mews", once led to the ten early cottages of Margaret Row, and into the old triangular stabling area for Burton Crescent (now Cartwright Gardens, p 97), covered long ago by an Express Dairies distribution depot. The **Lord John Russell** pub honours (according to its sign) the third son of the 6th Duke of Bedford, prime minister in 1846-52. However, the pub's landlord in the 1850s was a Mr John Russell. Was there, perhaps, something tongue-in-cheek about its naming? Was he cocking a snook at the Duke, from whose neighbouring estate public houses were largely excluded?

Turn south along the east side of the

street's central section, surprisingly leafy in summer. Older houses survive on the west side. **No.67**, once a butcher's, where a donkey in the basement trod a wheel to make sausage meat. **Nos.69&71** carry metal plates (SGB 1817/SPP 1791) testifying both to the antiquity of the premises and to the position of the old parish boundary. On the left note the gay and lesbian bookshop 'Gay's the Word' and the Marchmont Street Community Centre, being repaired in 2008 with lottery funding. Opposite at **No.55**, the distinguished potter Mick Casson (1925–2003), who devised and presented the ground-breaking series *The Craft of the Potter* (1975) for the BBC, opened a basement studio with an electric kiln, in 1952. Next door at **No.57** the comic actor Kenneth Williams lived as a child and until he was 30, above a hairdresser's managed by his father; the present occupiers, CV Hair & Beauty, are still in a similar line of business. A temporary neighbour of the Williamses was a youthful Richard Greene, later star of the 1950s TV series *Robin Hood*, who lived in a Marchmont Street flat in 1937, while working as a film extra and appearing in advertisements for shirts, hats, riding-boots and Brylcreem. At **No.43** (then No.7) watercolour painter John Skinner Prout lived in 1838-40 and No.41 (then No.6) was home to St Giles-born painter William Henry (Bird's Nest) Hunt from 1825. **No.39** bears an unofficial plaque to the American writer Charles Hoy Fort, who lived here in 1920-21 and who founded Forteanism, the study of "anomalous phenomena". The **Marquess of Cornwallis** pub beyond has reverted to its traditional name after a decade as part of the Goose (& Granite) chain. Note the finely carved coat of arms on the façade, with the motto 'virtus vincit invidiam' (virtue overcomes envy); and on the corner the gilt-framed glazed portrait of the 1st Marquess, a hero of the American War of Independence, victorious in 1780 at the Battle of Camden (South Carolina!).

In 1877-78 Marchmont Street absorbed Everett Street (after Thomas Everett, FH vice-president 1797-1810), ahead to the south and now wholly modern. At No.6 Everett Street (later No.11 Marchmont Street), lived James Poole, a linen draper who became a high-class West End tailor, and pioneered the Savile Row suit of clothes. However, his son Henry is often credited as being the 'Founder of Savile Row' after opening a second entrance to his late father's tailoring premises in 1846.

Follow unlabelled 'Coram Arcade' eastward into **The Brunswick**, until recently known as the Brunswick Centre, and on reaching its central piazza turn right. The multi-storey development of shops and Camden Council flats was erected by Marchmont Properties, a McAlpine subsidiary. First mooted in 1958, the scheme came to fruition only in 1969-72, in the wake of several abortive earlier plans. Designed by Patrick Hodgkinson, the complex has been praised and criticised in equal measure, acclaimed by some as "bold and uncompromising", and compared by others to everything from a gun emplacement to a nuclear power station. Though it has been often described as a 'megastructure', Hodgkinson disliked the term. Shops and eating places line a central (pedestrian) piazza, conceived by the architect as a 'village street'. Rising above on either side are the A-frame stepped-back terraces of two long blocks of flats – **Foundling Court** and **O'Donnell Court** – the latter named after Dr J J O'Donnell, a philanthropic local GP of the early 20th century. The greenhouses fronting each flat, and The Brunswick's defining feature, were originally conceived as larger 'winter gardens' but were scaled down to leave room for the open balconies that the Council prescribed. Run-down by 1999, and taken over by Allied London Properties, the centre gained Grade-II Listed status in the following year. Hodgkinson was invited to return and redevelop his earlier work. In a major refurbishment, completed in 2006, the concrete was painted cream, as the architect had originally wished. The piazza's crudely columned colonnades have given way to more delicate canopies. A west-facing Safeways (latterly Morrisons) supermarket has been replaced by a south-facing Waitrose which blocks public access from the north. With its smart shops and pavement cafés, The Brunswick has gained a new vibrancy unimaginable a decade ago, though the dearth of small independent outlets is disappointing. Next to the centre's Brunswick Square 'portal' is the subterranean **Renoir** cinema, so renamed in 1986 after the French film director. First opened as the Bloomsbury in 1972, and after several changes of ownership and five changes of name, it still thrives, specialising in independent, classic and foreign films.

Leave the precinct at the south end and descend into **BERNARD STREET**; staying on the northern pavement, walk west. The street was built by James Burton in 1799-1820 and named after Sir Thomas Bernard, the FH vice-president in 1806. It opened onto Russell Square by arrangement with the Duke of Bedford. Old houses remain on the opposite side, and first look east to **No.28**, all of eight bays wide, as it comprises Nos.25-28, knocked into one to form a hotel known in the 1930s as Mackenzie's. In 1928 No.26 was a second home of Rev. Harold Davidson, Rector of Stiffkey (Norfolk), who spent his weekends serving his parishioners, his weekdays and nights in London "saving fallen women". Allegations that he was saving them for his own pleasure led to his being sensationally defrocked in 1932, after which he became a seaside sideshow attraction, and, in the Biblical role of Daniel, was eventually mauled to death by a lion. **Nos.11-24** show great variety in the size and shape of their balconies.

On the north side none of the original houses survive. The Brunswick Centre engulfed erstwhile No.39, home in 1808-43 of Dr Peter Mark Roget, physician and polymath, founder of the Society for the Diffusion of Useful Knowledge, lecturer at the Russell Institution (p 62) and Secretary of the Royal Society 1827-49. Only upon retirement at the age of seventy did he embark on his well-known *Thesaurus of English Words and Phrases* (first edition 1852). Farther east, **No.40** was erected by Sir Robert McAlpine Ltd, builders of the adjacent hotel and shopping centre, to serve as its own headquarters. At No.48, on this site, artist Roger Fry (d.1934) spent his last years with Helen, the wife of mosaicist Boris Anrep. Ahead on the left, at No.2 on the Hotel Russell site, Joseph Munden, the celebrated Holborn-born comic actor, died in 1832.

Nearby is **Russell Square Station**, opened in 1906 on the Great Northern, Piccadilly & Brompton Railway. Admire the 1990s restoration of Leslie Green's oxblood-tiled exterior before, perhaps, venturing inside for your transport home.

Route 7
The Calthorpe estate and the Fleet valley
Circular walk from the Eastman Dental Hospital
(see back cover for map)

This walk begins and ends at the bus stop outside the Eastman Dental Hospital in **GRAY'S INN ROAD**. Just north of the hospital is the interesting split-level garden of the Calthorpe Project, to which we shall return at the end of the walk. Its name relates to the Calthorpe estate, in the northern half of which it lies. In 1706 Richard Gough, a wool merchant, bought three fields in the old manor of Portpool, which by the later 18th century had been leased to Daniel Harrison for the excavation of brick-earth. Here, we would be in the northern part of Gough's 'Middlefield'. Richard's son married into the Calthorpe family, and his grandson George, the 3rd Baron, was largely responsible for developing the estate after an Act was passed in 1814 to enable him to grant building leases. The Project garden occupies the site of Cubitt's yard, the local base of Thomas Cubitt, the remarkable builder who revolutionised the building industry by employing a permanent skilled workforce. Employed here c.1840 was William Edmund Davies, a bookmaker who was known as "The Leviathan" for the size of his personal bets,

which often amounted to £1,000. Opened soon after 1815, the yard here, from which much of Bloomsbury (to the west) was built, eventually expanded eastwards to Cubitt Street (p 73) and beyond. The family firm merged in Edwardian times with Bloomsbury-based builders Hannen & Holland, remaining in Gray's Inn Road until the 1960s.

Walk briefly north along Gray's Inn Road, which was lined here from the early 1820s by the houses and shops of Calthorpe Place. At No.4 William Thomas Lowndes, bibliographer, known within the trade for "bibliographical drudgery" and who wrote *The Bibliographer's Manual* (1834) in fifteen parts, which "reduced him to a wreck", lived at the end of his life in 1843.

Turn right (east) down residential **FREDERICK STREET**. Literally down, for we are now dropping perceptibly into the valley of the Fleet river. Frederick was the Christian name of the 4th and 5th Barons Calthorpe. The street is almost intact and variations in style and height suggest gradual development. The western part of the street (1823-27) was built by Thomas Cubitt, the later eastern end (1827-39) by his brother William, the future Lord Mayor of London. The street was originally protected from public traffic by bar gates, removed in 1893; however, although it began as a middle-class haven, by the time of Charles Booth's poverty map (c.1889) its inhabitants were categorised as comfortable working class. Frederick Street was very briefly the residence of Lenin in 1902, presaging the occupation of many addresses in the general area by Communist or Leftist organisations. Earlier, Thomas Carlyle stayed for a while at **No.47** on the right-hand side. Further along at **No.31** Bruce Bernard (1928-2000), photographer, writer, picture editor of *The Sunday Times*, and friend of artists Francis Bacon and Lucien Freud, lived and died. He wrote a biography of Bacon over which they quarrelled, and consequently it was never published. Pause at the corner and look across at Thomas Cubitt's showpiece at **Nos.48-52**, which have iron canopies above unusually large first-floor windows, facing short **AMPTON PLACE**, into which we turn. Its few houses were built by William Cubitt only in 1845-47 and it was known as Frederick Place until 1937.

We soon reach **AMPTON STREET**, named after a country seat of the Calthorpes in Suffolk. Barred against through traffic, this quiet street also retains most of its original houses. **Nos.18-36** and **21-39** at the west end – to our right – are the earliest (Thomas Cubitt, 1819-23). In 1831 Thomas and Jane Carlyle lodged for six months at **No.33** (then No.4) with a family of Irvingites. This was their first home in London, where Carlyle wrote an essay on Johnson. They returned here in 1834 (LCC brown plaque), before moving to Chelsea.

Set in the northern pavement is a varied selection of florid coal-hole covers from several different local suppliers. **Nos.11-19**, built after 1835 by William Cubitt, have strikingly sturdy pedimented porticoes, surmounted by black scallops. Booth walked the area in June 1898 to update his poverty map and noted that Ampton Street had declined somewhat and had become full of lodging houses.

Turn left to follow the lower, pedestrianised, end of the street, known as Ampton Place until 1885. It penetrates a modern development of low-rise brick-faced Council housing. To your right, with historically relevant names and barred to outsiders are **FLEET SQUARE** and **WELLS SQUARE**, approached from the south by **SEDDON STREET**. On the left is **SAGE WAY**. The last two names derive from the works in Gray's Inn Road of the Seddon family (p 80), and from Frederick Sage (b.1777), who built up a huge shop-fitting business, just south of our area.

Turn left into **CUBITT STREET**, which was Arthur Street until 1894. It originally continued south to Wren Street, along what is now Langton Close, until bisected by the eastward expansion of Cubitt's yard and diverted into King's Cross Road. On the east side, new private housing occupies a site that once contained a GPO depot, earlier a garage (destroyed in WWII), and very much earlier the pleasure gardens of Bagnigge Wells (see later). At the north-eastern corner of the street is the former Arthur Street Baptist Chapel (later Ampton Street Baptist Church). This was built in 1861 for an oddly peripatetic congregation which had previously worshipped in Whitechapel, Aldersgate, Moorfields and Spitalfields. They must have settled down in Arthur Street, for they were still here a century later. In 1950, the war-damaged chapel was acquired by the Field Lane Foundation, a charity with its origins in the Field Lane Ragged School, Saffron Hill. Its pioneering day centre for the elderly flourished here from 1952 to 1996. It became the Siddha Yoga Meditation Centre and is now the base for the Only Connect theatre for ex-offenders.

Past the chapel, regain **FREDERICK STREET**. Turn right along it, noting opposite the steeply sloping **Frederick Street Garden**, for local community use, on the site of former Nos.4-10. Beyond is the **Carpenters' Arms** on the corner of **KING'S CROSS ROAD**, along which we now proceed southward by turning right. The present name superseded the earlier Bagnigge Wells Road in 1863; earlier still it was known as the Lower Road, since it followed the once steep-sided valley of the Fleet. The river flowed a little to the west of it, on the way south from its sources at Hampstead and Highgate to join the Thames at Blackfriars. Though once a fast-flowing stream, fed by several local springs, it had by 1850 become an open sewer, soon to be condemned to an underground existence as part of the Victorian sewerage system. The Camden-Islington boundary runs along the middle of King's Cross Road, of which only the western side concerns us here, although the walker should look over the road to see the splendid former police station (now traffic wardens' centre), in the Borough of Islington.

The site of Nos.71-101 on the Camden side was first developed in the late 18th century as Pearl Crescent, on waste ground held copyhold of the Manor of Cantelowes. The houses, several of which were shops, were frequently inundated by the Fleet, a particularly bad flood occurring in May 1818. In 1843 the boot and shoe maker William Haggett was admonished by the local magistrate for treating his apprentice like a slave, allowing him only 5-minute breaks to eat meals taken at his workbench. None of the early buildings of Pearl Crescent have survived. A former petrol station was in 2008 making way for new apartments. Beyond is **Phoenix Yard**, industrial buildings converted to offices, including those of the architects Shepheard Epstein Hunter.

There then begins a terrace of early Victorian houses. Between **Nos.61** and **No.63** – just behind a bus stop – is a small stone plaque, salvaged from an old boundary wall, comprising a keystone depicting a mask, and the inscription:

S + T
THIS IS BAGNIGGE
HOVSE NEARE
THE PINDER A
WAKEFEILDE
1680

The letters have been recut, and 'ST' may have been a misreading of 'SP' (St Pancras). The 'Pinder' was a well-known hostelry in the Gray's Inn Road (p 105), Bagnigge (pronounced 'Bagnij') House a 17th-century residence, named after an

old local family. In 1757 land here was acquired by Thomas Hughes, a Holborn tobacconist. The story goes that, unable to grow anything in his garden, he sought advice from Dr John Bevis, a scientist and astronomer, who analysed the local water and declared it to be both rich in iron and with excellent purgative properties. So was born Bagnigge Wells **[22]**, among the most popular and fashionable of 18th-century spas, which Hughes opened to the public in 1759.

The gardens, which straddled the river, offered a grotto, fountain and fish pond, tea arbours and a bun house, a skittle alley and a bowling green. In the Long Room, an organ was available for concerts. By the 1770s it was regarded by City merchants and their wives as the very height of gentility:

Bon Ton's the space 'twixt Saturday and
    Monday;
And riding in a one-horse chair on Sunday;
    'Tis drinking tea on summer afternoons
At Bagnigge Wells with china and gilt
    spoons.

[Colman's prologue to Garrick's *Bon Ton*, 1775]

but by the 19th century the spa had

22 Bagnigge Wells, by R B Schnebbelie for George Daniel, c.1833

declined into a resort of the lower classes, and in 1841 it closed. Tradition has it (on no very good evidence) that Bagnigge House was a summer retreat of Nell Gwynne, where she threw wild parties, and entertained Charles II with "little concerts and breakfasts". Although the house once boasted a bust of Nell, supposedly by Sir Peter Lely, it could well have simply been placed there by Hughes as an attraction. We nevertheless have Gwynne Place, on the Islington side of the road, spanned by the upper storeys of the modern **London Farringdon Travelodge**. It leads to the nameless ascent to Granville Square immortalised in Arnold Bennett's *Riceyman's Steps* (1924), a novel which vividly portrays the district, aptly likening King's Cross Road to a "canyon". On the corner ahead, where we pause, a recent block of flats at **No.2 Cubitt Street** marks the location of the Bagnigge Wells Tavern, built on the site of the spa's entertainment centre, licensed as a theatre from 1848 to 1874, and closed in the early years of WWII.

The large hotel beyond stands on what were once Cold Bath Fields. Early houses built here, forming Brook Place, were swept away to make way for Rowton House, one of several London hostels founded by Lord Rowton to provide cheap, basic accommodation for working-class men. Opened in 1894 with 678 beds, it eventually closed in 1960, reopening the

following year as the Mount Pleasant Hotel. The massive red-brick **Holiday Inn** now covers the site, serving an altogether better-heeled class of transients. Much water has flowed under erstwhile Black Mary's Bridge since Rocque's map of 1746 identified the hamlet here as Black Mary's Hole. The eponymous Mary may have been a 'blackmoor woman' who had lived by the road (c.1720) in a circular stone-built hut, although Peter Ackroyd claims that in medieval times this spot was known as Blessed Mary's Well and was renamed after the Reformation.

We now turn right along the southern spur of **CUBITT STREET**. The modern Rollercoasters Play Centre at **No.3** extends onto the site of Model Buildings, where until the 1960s an alleyway was lined on one side by very small cottages designed by Henry Roberts in 1844-45 for the Society for Improving the Condition of the Labouring Classes. There were fourteen family houses and lodgings for "30 aged females", the latter becoming known as Widows' Buildings. This, the Society's first venture, was deemed a failure. The cramped environment was much criticised even at the time, and the embarrassed Society sold the property to one of its members after only ten years. By 1889 the street was another patch of "very poor" blue on Booth's map, although he upgraded this to a "mixed" purple in 1898, impressed by the fact that all the doors in the model dwellings were shut, the windows cleaned and decorated with flowers.

A left turn leads into **PAKENHAM STREET**; Pakenham was another Suffolk seat of the Calthorpes. On its east side is an original terrace of 2-storey houses, with an unusually wide band of unrelieved brickwork above the first floor windows. Opposite the southern end of the terrace is an old industrial building, with barred windows on the ground floor, which has served at various times as a depot of the London Improved Cab Co., as the garage of hauliers Carter Paterson, and as a dairy and bookbindery. It is now a part of Camden Council's **Wren Workshops** (here numbered No.23 Pakenham Street), currently occupied by Studio One Originations and Newman Display Ltd. At the time of writing (mid 2008) the adjoining light industrial unit at No.21 Wren Street was empty and the Council was considering a proposal to build a small secondary school there.

Following the street southwards, we become aware that although proceeding downstream, close to the old river bank, we are walking *up*hill! This is because the eastern end of Calthorpe Street (ahead) was built on artificially raised ground to avoid the kind of switchback observable farther south at Mount Pleasant.

Pause at the **Pakenham Arms** on the corner of Calthorpe Street. Opposite is **PHOENIX PLACE**, dropping towards the natural level of the valley floor, and here forming the modern Camden-Islington boundary, which has swung westwards following a meander in the course of the river. Another of the Fleet's several names was Turnmill Brook, and its banks hereabouts were once a hive of light industry. The street's name may have alluded to its having risen 'out of the ashes' of the large dust heap which had once occupied the lower end of the slope. 19th-century Phoenix Place was home to colonies of wood turners and glass cutters, to the barrel-organ works of Pasquale & Co., and to the Phoenix Brass Foundry which stood at its southern end until seriously damaged in WWII. Houses were built only along the west side, where just one building remains; otherwise, all is desolation. To the east, and now wholly in Islington, is the huge Mount Pleasant sorting depot of the Royal Mail. Opened in 1889 as the Parcel Post Office, it occupies the site of the notoriously harsh Cold Bath Fields Prison, or Middlesex House of Correction (1794-1877).

CALTHORPE STREET, an extension of Guilford Street, was developed in three stages. The latest built eastern end, to the left of the corner on which you are standing, was called Lower Calthorpe Street before 1876. Camden Council's School House Workshops at **No.51** occupy a mid-19th century building, originally a school of the (nonconformist) British & Foreign Schools Society. It later served, before WWI, as a drill hall of the Royal Army Medical Corps (Volunteers). Abutting it is Grade-II-Listed **No.49**, which achieved brief notoriety in 2004 when an artists' collective that had squatted in it since 1973 gained the freehold; it was then valued at £1m. The one-storey building opposite us, **No.50**, with its rusticated quoins, has a disappointingly mundane past, having served for half a century as a tobacconist's and now used as offices.

Cross over to it and walk west along the central section of the street, which consists of half-stuccoed 3-storey houses of 1842-49. Pause at the corner of Gough Street and look along the earliest built west end of the street (1821-26), where Sir Joseph William Chitty was born in 1828. He was known behind his back as "Mr Justice Chatty" for his habit of engaging in conversation with counsel in court. One of these 4-storey terraced houses, **No.20**, bears a blue plaque recording the residence in 1880-91 of the architect William Lethaby, founder of the Art Workers' Guild (p 32). Nathaniel Stallwood, the wealthy developer of this end of the street, lived at **No.21** on the corner of Gough Street. From his large balcony, now demolished, on the Gough Street frontage he witnessed the so-called Clerkenwell Riot of Monday 13 May 1833. A meeting of the unemployed, in support of working-class suffrage, took place in Cold Bath Fields. Banned by the authorities, it was brutally dispersed by contingents of the newly formed police. As the ensuing affray spread into surrounding streets, PC Culley was stabbed on the pavement in Calthorpe Street, staggered to the yard of the Calthorpe Arms in Gray's Inn Road, and died. This is often said to have been the first ever killing of a constable on duty. The coroner's inquest became a *cause célèbre* when a jury sympathetic to the rioters returned a verdict of justifiable homicide, since the police had baton-charged the crowd without first reading the Riot Act.

Diagonally opposite No.21, **No.26** was the home from 1862 to 1911 of George Hare, an early maker of photographic equipment. It was previously occupied by Joseph Wright, co-founder of Wright & Horne, London's largest coach-building business, which in 1835 won the contract to supply most of the first-class mail coaches to the Royal Mail. The factory (c.1812) adjoining his house extended from **GOUGH STREET** to the river bank, and made omnibuses as well as coaches until it closed in 1852. The vacated space served later as stables. Booth noted in 1898 that it contained 200 cabs owned by Hearn. It was known as Royal Mail Yard; now it is mainly parking space.

Turn left down Gough Street to pass it. Beyond, houses at Nos.42-50 survived until the 1950s; part of their fronts remains, with the entrances and windows bricked up and serving now as a wall. No trace survives, however, of the Two Brewers pub that adjoined them at No.52 which was demolished a few years later. The backs of ultramodern office blocks in the Gray's Inn Road line the opposite side of the incongruously cobbled street.

On the right is **COLEY STREET** which we enter, just short of the old St Pancras-Holborn boundary. It was known as Wilson Street until 1935, when it was renamed after Henry Coley, a 17th-century astrologer who lived in Baldwin's Gardens in Holborn, to the south. On the corner of Gough and Wilson Streets stood an establishment successively known as Pym's Private Theatre, as the Amateurs' Subscription Theatre (by 1832), and 20 years later as the Dramatic Institution & School for the Stage. Here the young actor Edwin John James frequently acted. He gave up acting to become a barrister and eventually a QC. He defended William Palmer, the "Rugeley Poisoner" in 1856 and the would-be assassins of Napoleon III.

Between Nos.3&4 in the middle of the south side an arch once led to the cramped and airless Wilson Place. "Mark it as black as you can" exhorted Booth in 1898, because he considered it a colony of Irish thieves, who regularly assaulted the police. Conditions in the cul-de-sac, which abutted a timber works, were unsavoury; a labourer's daughter, aged five, died here in July 1867 of "choleraic diarrhoea". Wilson Place was cleared after WWI to become the site of Kemsley House (see below).

We soon rejoin **GRAY'S INN ROAD**. This was part of an ancient route to the north from the City markets, known originally as Portpoole Lane, but by Tudor times as Gray's Inn Lane. In 1660 General Monck marched 5800 troops along it to billets in Holborn, with the aim of restoring the monarchy; and in Fielding's *Tom Jones* the eponymous hero enters London by the same route. By the 18th century the east side had been built up as far as where you stand, while development at the northern (King's Cross) end began in the 1760s. The intervening stretch was built up in the first half of the next century, along with the estates bordering it on either side. Gray's Inn Road has often been described as 'dreary', with no real sense of purpose, and for this its unplanned, piecemeal development must be partly to blame. In 1862 the Lane officially became a Road, and the separately numbered terraces lining it were integrated within a single numbering scheme. The roadway was doubled in width by the Metropolitan Board of Works in 1879-80, and a decade later the London Street Tramways Co. laid a tramway along it to run from King's Cross to a terminus at Holborn Hall.

The Coley Street corner is bounded

by modern blocks, each recalling the thoroughfare's long association with the news media. To the south at **No.200** is the glassy 1986 headquarters of Independent Television News, designed by Norman Foster, its atrium descending into the basement area which once housed the giant presses of former Kemsley House, pre-WWII printing works of Allied Newspapers. James Gomer Berry, first Viscount Kemsley, newspaper proprietor and owner of the *Sunday Times* (1915), *Financial Times* (1919), and *The Daily Telegraph* (1927), *The Daily Sketch* and *The Sunday Graphic,* lived at the former No.200. Kemsley House was known as Thomson House from the late 1950s until its demolition.

Turn north past **Nos.222-236,** a long, mellower, arcaded block designed by Richard Seifert & Partners, built by McAlpine in 1974 for the Times newspaper group. Then named "New Printing House Square", after the Thunderer's traditional City base, it housed *The Times* and *Sunday Times* until their departure for Wapping in 1986.

The building covers the site of St Bartholomew's, a very plain church of 1811, built as Providence Chapel for a coalheaver and preacher called William Huntingdon, SS (for 'Sinner Saved'). It was subsequently altered and opened as a Proprietary Episcopal Church by Rev. Thomas Mortimer in April 1837, and

became a District Church in 1860. Eighty years later it was virtually destroyed by a bomb, and its site was used as a car-park and subsequently a garage before 'New Printing House Square' was erected.

North of the chapel once stood Leader's Coach & City Cavalry Stables, built in Old Merchant's Field, Gough's southernmost meadow, but swept away in the building of Calthorpe Street. The **Blue Lion,** on the west side of Gray's Inn Road, was relocated from the east side when its site was needed for building. The earlier tavern had been nicknamed the 'Blue Cat' in mockery of its ill-painted sign. A Blue Lion Yard remained off the east side, becoming the long-time premises of Patrick Hearn, "job master" in the 19th century and road haulier in the next. The bizarre single-storey building, a former high-class bed shop, at **No.238A** is a modern creation. It occupies the original site of the Central London Ophthalmic Hospital from 1843 until the latter moved to Judd Street (p 92).

Continue northwards as far as the **Calthorpe Arms,** which dates from c.1826, and retains its wood-framed windows. Here PC Culley died, and the subsequent inquest was held. Note the authentic Calthorpe coat of arms on the pub-sign, supported by two heraldic 'savages' – near-naked (white) bearded men wielding clubs and with only sprigs of oak leaves to preserve their modesty.

Turn right into **WREN STREET,** built

progressively from 1824 to 1849. Since it approached the former spa it was called Wells Street until 1937, when it was named after the architect, a one-time resident of Bloomsbury. On the south side most of the original houses remain, 3-storeyed at the earlier western end with attractive ironwork, reducing to 2 storeys further east. No.10 was demolished after WWII and on its site was built **No.50 Gough Street,** which gives access to **GREEN YARD,** where a mixed development of mews-style flats and houses was built 1989-91 by the St Pancras Housing Association. Several properties were let to homeless families. On this site stood the Victorian cabinet factory of Viscardini Baldassare, which remained in the same line of business through the interwar period.

On the east corner of Gough Street is a striped St Pancras Parish bollard, and in front of it an old stone one. At the bend in the road beyond, the line of the frontage is preserved by an unusual free-standing stuccoed wall, pierced by two rounded arches serving as entrances to **Nos.15-16.** Opposite is **LANGTON CLOSE,** named after the Arthur Langton Nurses' Home on the west side (related to the adjacent former Royal Free Hospital), which was refurbished in 1995 as a hostel for students of University College. The houses that were on the site were earlier numbered as part of Cubitt Street.

23 St David's Day, 1845. Boys processing from the Welsh Charity School, Gray's Inn Road, sporting leeks in their military-style caps

Cross over to the entrance to pleasant but under-used **St Andrew's Gardens**, through which we now pass by taking the path diagonally across it. The land here was acquired under a 1746 Act and consecrated in 1754 as an overspill burial ground for St Andrew's Holborn. Buried here was the Chevalier John Theodora de Verdion, a once well-known London bookseller, who lived in London as a man, but had in fact been born as a woman. This was only discovered after her death from breast cancer aged 58 in 1802. Here were reburied the bones of the teenage poet Thomas Chatterton, and those of paupers from the Shoe Lane workhouse. Like the nearby St George's Gardens (p 66), the site was laid out as a public park in 1885 by St Pancras Vestry; here too there is a drinking fountain donated by Emily Bessie Orbell (p 67). We pass another plaque on the wall of the garden informing us that the gardens were opened by Lady John Manners.

We come back into **GRAY'S INN ROAD** by **Trinity Court**, a 9-storey block of flats in concrete, with angular balconies, built in 1935. It stands on the site of Holy Trinity Church, a Grecian-style edifice, built in 1837-39 by James Pennethorne as a chapel-of-ease to St Andrew's Holborn, with seats for 1500 souls, and catacombs beneath for 1000 bodies. It was restored in 1880, but closed in 1928, when the parish merged with that of St George the Martyr. In 1873 a school designed in neo-Gothic style by

Charles H Cooke was erected south of the church, built on arches to avoid disturbance to the graveyard. With the opening of the Prospect Terrace schools (p 108) in 1882 it became redundant. Its building survives (as offices), at **No.252** to your left, also known as Sphinx House.

Before turning north, look at **Nos.141-153** on the opposite (west) side of the road. They are a few surviving houses in what was originally Foundling Terrace, where at No.2½ the organ builder Henry ('Father') Willis opened his first shop in 1848-50. Yellow-bricked **No.155**, spanning the entrance to a one-time signmaker's yard, and long occupied by Barnes & Mullins, makers and subsequently wholesalers of musical instruments, is now occupied by John Laing Training. The neighbouring **Canolfan Llundain Cymry** (London Welsh Centre) houses an association dedicated to the promotion of the Welsh language. Dating from before WWII, it was home during the war to the Welsh Services Club. Almost opposite, north of the old graveyard, once stood the Welsh Charity School **[23]**, founded in 1718 for the "education and welfare of poor children of Welsh parents born in or near London". The school moved here from Clerkenwell Green in 1772, departing 85 years later for Ashford, Middlesex where, as St David's School, it still exists. The Gray's Inn Road site was later occupied by Eley Bros. ammunition factory, scene of a

fatal explosion in 1900; the company refused admission to the Goad insurance map makers soon after. Part of it subsequently reverted to more humanitarian use as a British Legion poppy warehouse.

North of the Centre, at **No.167**, are the flats of **Jubilee House**, opened in 1985 to celebrate the 50th anniversary of the National Federation of Housing Associations, whose headquarters used to be next door at **No.171**. To the north, in front of a row of old houses once known as Mecklenburgh Terrace but now fronted by a modern showroom, is a granite horse trough erected in 1885 by the Metropolitan Drinking Fountain & Cattle Trough Association, inscribed with two apposite biblical texts, and some cryptic initials, presumably those of people related to the donor, a Mr E G Wood.

On the east side of the road is the extensive site once occupied by the Royal Free Hospital. The first building here was the barracks built in 1812 for the Light Horse Volunteers, consisting of four blocks around a square courtyard, which remains and is worth a closer look. For a decade from 1832, the blocks housed the factory of Thomas and George Seddon, cabinet makers and upholsterers, where Regency-style furniture was made. Their furniture is identifiable by the paper notes attached to the underside of each piece. In 1843 the Free Hospital, by now under royal patronage, moved from Hatton Garden into the old barracks, to provide more beds. The northern Sussex Wing **[24]** was added in 1856, followed by the Victoria Wing (1878) to the rear and, in 1895, the Alexandra Building, a splendid neoclassical block fronting Gray's Inn Road, its pediment adorned by the royal arms. In 1877 the Royal Free was the first hospital to admit female medical students; in 1895

24 The Royal Free Hospital, c.1856, 'showing the new Sussex Wing'

it appointed the first Lady Almoner; and in 1921 opened England's first obstetrics and gynaecology unit. In 1926-30 the **Eastman Dental Hospital** was constructed on the charity school site to the south, designed by Burnet, Tait & Lorne, and sponsored by the American George Eastman, of Eastman-Kodak fame. After the removal of the Royal Free to Hampstead in c.1974, the main block served as offices of the Area Health Authority; the dental hospital has now expanded to fill the whole complex, in company with London University's Institute of Dental Surgery, as well as the Assisted Conception Unit.

So we have come full circle. Buses running north and south stop nearby but before catching one, spend some time in the adjoining **Calthorpe Project**. This was opened in 1984 on land saved from office development by a spirited public campaign, and cared for by local community groups (present opening times variable). Do not miss the numerous murals painted on the side wall of the hospital.

Route 8
South east of King's Cross
Circular walk from King's Cross
(see back cover for map)

With **King's Cross** mainline station behind you, imagine the scene here three centuries ago when this was all open country. An old road ran north from Holborn along the lines of modern Gray's Inn and Pancras Roads; and a short distance in front of where you stand it crossed the Fleet river over a single brick arch called Battle Bridge. 'Battle' is probably a corruption of Bradford (or Broad Ford), perhaps how the river was crossed in earlier times. Tales that this was the site of a battle between Boudicca and the Romans, or between Alfred and the Danes, are wholly unfounded.

Local developers in the early 19th century wanted the area renamed to improve its image, long tarnished by the presence of Smith's dust heap at the top end of Gray's Inn Road (p 76) and the Smallpox Hospital which lay just to the west of the station site. Early suggestions included Boadicea's Cross, Pancras Cross and St George's Cross. *The Times* in February 1830 reported that Battlebridge was undergoing a huge improvement, changing from a filthy and dangerous

location, and that Robert Peel had ordered that a unit of the new police force would be housed at the junction of the roads to be renamed St George's Cross. At the same time Stephen Geary, architect of the Panarmonion (p 103), proposed that a monument be built, with a police station in its base and above it a statue of George IV, to be paid for by public subscription. But the monarch inconveniently died, and by 1835 only enough money had been raised for a third-rate statue, hastily sculpted *in situ* from builder's composition while it dried. The police had meanwhile moved into the statueless base in 1831; when they outgrew their cramped station and left, it became a beershop. Continually mocked and satirised, and ill-lit at night, the 40ft-high monument was declared a public nuisance in 1845, and summarily demolished by the Vestry. The statue had meanwhile given its name not only to the junction (called King's Cross Circus) but to the surrounding area of Battlebridge, although the old name was still being used as an alternative to "King's Cross" even after the station was opened in 1852.

Until about 1834 the acute angle between Gray's Inn and Pentonville Roads was occupied by a rustic tavern called the White Hart (**[25]**, p 83) licensed since at least 1721. A grander replacement, in more urban style and surmounted by a squat tower, but still semi-circular in form, was short-lived. In c.1860 the whole peninsular site was cleared for the construction of the underground Metropolitan Railway, to be refilled in 1873-74 by the 4-storey Italianate block popularly known as the **Lighthouse Building**. Above the corner is a peculiar metal-clad wooden structure resembling a lighthouse, which until 1978 was largely obscured by advertising hoardings. Their removal prompted many ingenious theories as to the origins and purpose of the tower which, despite the best endeavours of local historians, remain a mystery. All that can be said with virtual certainty is that the tower served no practical purpose, but was a folly or architectural conceit intended to emphasise the importance of this junction of seven major roads - or possibly to enhance the marketability of a building erected

25 Battlebridge, 1814: the White Hart public house on the King's Cross 'Lighthouse Building' site

directly over the railway tunnels, and thus much prone to noise and vibration. At present the building awaits refurbishment. A scheme in 2002 for new shops and restaurants, as part of P&O's Regent Quarter development on the north side of **PENTONVILLE ROAD,** was abandoned.

To our left, we cross over by the lights to this north, Islington, side of the street, the better to view the south, Camden side. The latter was first developed in the late 18th century as Cumberland Row, none of which survives. **KING'S CROSS BRIDGE** (on the right) was constructed in 1910-12 to enable trams to run from the Caledonian Road without having to negotiate a very sharp curve at the 'lighthouse' corner. Although tramways were excluded from most of Central London, horse-drawn cars of the London Street Tramway Co. did penetrate down both King's Cross and Gray's Inn Roads from 1889, to terminate at Farringdon or Holborn. The tramway was taken over by the LCC in 1906 and electrified in 1911-12. King's Cross Bridge spanned the tracks of the Metropolitan Railway, the world's first underground line, opened between Paddington and Farringdon in 1863 and initially served by steam locomotives. The original street-level buildings of the Metropolitan's King's Cross station faced both Gray's Inn Road and Pentonville Road, but they were demolished and replaced shortly before WWI by a new station entrance on the west

side of the bridge. Although the structure still stands (minus its canopy), this entrance closed in 1941, when new platforms were opened beneath Euston Road, the original station having been destroyed in an air raid the year before. Boarded up, the entrance is labelled "London Regional Transport Catering Services Management".

Above the east side of King's Cross Bridge is the cupola of a former cinema, built in concrete on girders over the railway. The stuccoed baroque edifice, designed by H Courtney Constantine for the builder Abraham Davis (see p 92), was started in 1914 but completed only after WWI, during which it was used to make aeroplane components and later served as a demob centre. Opened in April 1920 as the King's Cross Cinema, it became the Gaumont in 1952, and ten years later the Odeon, closing under that name in 1970. It reopened a year later, reverting to its original name, and additionally running late-night rock shows until its licence was revoked following petitions from local residents. In 1980 it played host to the Primatrium, a short-lived audio-visual ecological experience, while part of the building became a snooker club and offices. In 1981 the circle seats reopened as the Scala Cinema Club, showing art-house films until 1993, when it went into receivership after an illegal showing of *A Clockwork Orange*. The Scala then became a nightclub, but a radical transformation, with two new floors added, led to its reopening as a multi-purpose venue with bars, dance floors and a stage for live music and other performances.

Beyond the bridge, in **PENTONVILLE ROAD**, is the glass-fronted former Thameslink station, which opened in 1983 as 'King's Cross Midland City', and occupies part of the site of the original Metropolitan station. Trains use the so-called 'Widened Lines', an extra pair of tracks built in 1868 to allow Midland and Great Northern trains to reach the City, and South London via Blackfriars. From 9 December 2007 trains switched to two new platforms built under St Pancras International, although the useful pedestrian tunnel to King's Cross and St Pancras remains open.

Beyond the station, the **Big Chill House** (Nos.257&259) was previously the Bell public house, a classically styled early gin palace often attributed to the architect Stephen Geary (p 82), who ironically became a staunch supporter of the Temperance movement. The building dates from c.1850 when it replaced an earlier Bell. It has been thoroughly modernised inside, with three floors and a terrace. It is run by the company that organise Big Chill, a popular annual music festival founded in 1994.

By the Poor School (of acting) cross over to the south-western side of **KING'S CROSS ROAD**, which veers off to the right.

For much of its length this side is lined by mid-19th-century 3-storey houses, most with shops or places of refreshment on the ground floor. They are interspersed with 20th-century replacements such as Nos.207-215, **Instrument House**, named after its first occupants Research and Control Instruments Ltd. It was home in the 1990s to various voluntary groups, who left in 2000 when Camden Council took over the building. It now houses a surgery and a psychotherapy unit. In the early-19th-century frontage beyond, first built as Field Terrace, some attractive shop fronts survive, such as those at **No.205**, where the barber's 'Saloon' has a splendid gold-lettered fascia; and at **Nos.193&195**, premises of Dodd's the Printers, a firm long established on this site.

By the side of Dodd's, turn through an archway that leads (right) into **ST CHAD'S PLACE**. This eastern end was until 1886 called Fifteen Foot Lane. The building with a cute lion's head above its doorway is all that remains of a Victorian tenement block called Stanley House, hence the sign on its side wall. This was the only site on this walk to be coloured deep blue (for 'very poor') on Booth's poverty map. In his notes taken in 1898 to update the map he records it as still rough, King's Cross being a haunt of prostitutes and including many courtyards that the police avoided entering. **No.6** was a derelict mechanic's workshop until restored by

its current owners, the architects Squire and Partners. Note the extensive glazing installed in the roof, which now lights a café, restaurant and bar in this original Victorian warehouse. Beyond it on the right lies the site of St Chad's Well, reputedly a medieval holy well, named for the patron saint of medicinal springs. By the late 18th century, it was a flourishing spa, 1,000 people a week taking the waters here in 1772, when an annual subscription cost £1. Its 'aperient' waters attracted many invalids. By early in the next century it had declined into a weekend pleasure garden for locals, and despite attempts to revitalise it, e.g. by building a theatre for equestrian events in 1829, the spa was soon to close. The property was sold in 1837; houses were built on the west side, and a schoolroom erected by the side of the old pumphouse. The old buildings and the remainder of the gardens were lost in the 1860s to the railway that follows the valley of the Fleet, which had flowed through the gardens. The railway goes southward in a cutting before tunnelling under a flank of Clerkenwell Hill.

Turning left beyond the railway bridge into **WICKLOW STREET**, we penetrate the area which was once the eastern half of Battle Bridge Field. In 1767 a carpenter named Richard Hedges leased land here for house building. Other local tradesmen followed suit, creating a suburb of small Georgian houses, of which the street pattern is today the only reminder. Most of the estate had been demolished by 1900, either to make way for the railway or to be replaced later by assorted light industry and warehousing. Heavily damaged in WWII, the still cobbled streets are now almost deserted outside working hours. The northern end of the street was known as Paradise Street until integrated with the southern part (former George Street) in 1886; why the combined street was named Wicklow is unknown.

On the left we pass a short stump (unlabelled) of **FIELD STREET**, which was a through route to King's Cross Road before the removal of its railway bridge, its far end visible beyond the cutting. In the 19th century a mission room of St Jude's church (p 88) existed on the north side close to the bridge at No.25. The street had its moment of fame as the spot where the getaway car was abandoned in *The Ladykillers*, Ealing Studios' black comedy of 1955. On its corner is **No.44 WICKLOW STREET**, now the headquarters of the General Chiropractic Council, the UK-wide regulatory body. It faces **No.77**, the rear of Pioneer House (p 89), which was refurbished in 2000-01 by the architects Squire & Partners to house their offices at ground floor level and 38 apartments in the floors above.

Turn left along **LEEKE STREET**, passing on the corner an old industrial building now partly occupied by **Smithy's** wine bar.

Originally this had been the site of Paradise Court, a close of small 18th-century houses. In the days of horse buses (c.1900) here were the stables of the London General Omnibus Company (LGOC); 20 years later the rival bus company of Thomas Tilling was in occupation, doubtless motorised by then, but sharing the address with an independent farrier. Taking-in doors at the Wicklow Street end of the L-shaped block were possibly associated with the building's later use as a chromium plating works. Beyond the railway **Nos.5-13** on our right, now housing a firm of public relations consultants, have a grimy façade, but note the inscription "1890" above the doorway, which is surmounted by a three-dimensional heraldic device: a gauntleted forearm with a sword hilt. It is perhaps no coincidence that a similar device serves as the crest of several families named Foster, and that the first occupiers of the building were Foster's Parcel Express Co. The building faces the European HQ of the Japanese store Muji.

On regaining King's Cross Road, observe on the far pavement two black metal posts inscribed "SPPM" (St Pancras Parish, Middlesex). Old photographs show identical posts lining the entire length of the road to mark the old limits of St Pancras and St James, Clerkenwell. The houses to our left were once Field Place, but we turn right along a stretch first known as Hertford Row, latterly Lion Terrace and then right

again into **BRITANNIA STREET**, the main thoroughfare of the early development in Battle Bridge Field. The patriotically named street was for many years flanked by George Street (after George III), from 1865 the southern arm of Wicklow Street, and by Charlotte Street, renamed Leeke Street in the same year. The **Golden Lion** pub, licensed as a theatre from 1854-64, was originally called the Golden Lions; the beasts involved were perhaps the heraldic ones of the royal arms. The corner of the building was once topped by a large statue of a lion. Opposite are the early **Nos.3&5**, before **Derby Lodge** (once Derby Buildings), a 'model' working-class tenement block in yellow stock brick, built in 1867-68 by the Improved Industrial Dwellings Company, and latterly managed by Camden Council. Booth noted in 1898 that it was full of the respectable working class such as policemen and cabmen, in contrast to the rest of the street which he characterised as poor, with house doors left open. Its outside stairwells and landings reflect a late preoccupation with through ventilation. Notice the diagonally patterned ironwork, repeated in Cobden Buildings, a companion block on the Islington side of King's Cross Road.

Derby Lodge faces the **Gagosian Gallery** at Nos.6-24, a contemporary art gallery, one of a chain of seven around the world owned by Larry Gagosian, which occupies the ground floor of the large block that has otherwise been refurbished as flats at No.26. On the far side of the bridge, **No.15** opposite is brick-built and bay-windowed, and houses the Writers' Guild of Great Britain, while on the northern side we pass **Nos.28-32**, the offices of Alfred McAlpine, housed in the original stables of the LGOC, whose name is inscribed above the entrance. Beyond, the corner block is Hospice House, formerly occupied by the Society of Graphical and Allied Trades, but now headquarters of the charity Help the Hospices. On the opposite corner, **No.27** houses the University and College Union Conference Centre. Dating from 1900, the premises were for over 80 years a bottled beer store and offices of Whitbread's, hence the deer's head (the brewery's trademark) above the door. The neo-Gothic Victorian building that faces it was formerly St Jude's National School; the associated church (p 88) has long been demolished. The radical Unity Theatre first opened in the redundant school in 1936, moving a year later to its better-known home in Goldington Street.

Turn left down **WICKLOW STREET**, and follow it round to the left as it passes the back of the Royal National Throat, Nose & Ear Hospital (p 88). Beyond the railway bridge on the left are further blocks of Derby Lodge, which overlook a small fenced play area first laid out in the 1960s. Behind it is a small building at **No.31A** with timber facing, called Wicklow

THE PATENT ROTARY HAIR BRUSH.

Mr. A. J. WILLIAMS begs to invite the attention of his Friends and the Public generally, to the newly invented ROTARY MACHINE BRUSH, which he has just erected in his spacious Hair Cutting Saloon. It is one of the very best of its kind, and insures perfect comfort and cleanliness, which are such important desiderata in the art of the *perruquier.*—Come and judge.

WILLIAMS' RESTORATIVE HAIR WASH.

This is an entirely NEW MEDICATED HAIR CLEANSER and PURIFIER, which will be found at once refreshing and invigorating during the process of SHAMPOOING. The clumsy, disagreeable, and antiquated method of Washing the Head in Water is entirely obviated by this new Invention of Mr. WILLIAMS.

WILLIAMS' TRICHALLASMATIST.

This is one of the most surprising discoveries of the time. After much patient labour and research, Mr. W. has succeeded in producing a liquid of marvellous efficacy in restoring the Human Hair to its original hue. Mr. W. guarantees that while his TRICHALLASMATIST will effect a complete metamorphosis in the colour of the Hair to a Natural Brown or Black, not the smallest trace of the pigment will be discovered on the surface of the scalp. One of the valuable properties of this chromatic is, that it will effect the transformation gradually at the option of the person applying it. Experience is better than precept. Come, try, and be convinced.—TESTIMONIALS can be seen at the Establishment.

In Bottles, 7s. 6d., 15s., and £1. 1s.

Inventor and Proprietor of the

TRICHOTROPHY, OR HAIR REGENERATOR.

Sold in Bottles, 2s. 6d., 5s. 6d., and 11s.

Gentlemen's Hair Cut on the most Improved principle, 3d. Shampooing, 4d. Cut and Shampooed (at the same time) 6d. Curling, 3d. Ladies' Hair Cut, 6d. Shampooed, 1s. Dressed, 6d.

Clean Brushes used to each Person.—Ladies and Gentlemen waited on at their own Residences.

SURGICAL INSTRUMENTS, and every description of CUTLERY, Ground, Set, and Repaired, on entirely new principles.

PLEASE NOTE THE ADDRESS:—

A. J. WILLIAMS, 121, KING'S CROSS ROAD.

M. Bowry & Son, Printers, 46, King's Cross Road.

26 Cutting-edge technology at No.121 King's Cross Road: undated hairdresser's advertisement

Mill. This was the HQ of the King's Cross Partnership, an organisation set up in 1997 to coordinate a seven-year Government-funded £37.5 million regeneration programme in King's Cross.

Adjoining the play area at **Nos.5-11** is a group of 3-storeyed Victorian double-fronted houses with an insistent design of triple windows. **No.1** is original, dating to the early 19th century, and retaining its yard entrance, which leads to outbuildings of the adjoining **Northumberland Arms** that turns the corner into **KING'S CROSS ROAD**. The pub had a theatre licence from before 1850 to 1874. The terrace to the north as far as Britannia Street bore the same name until 1865. We continue south past houses which were called Acton Place. At **No.133** was once another pub, the tiny Hansler Arms, which became Finnegan's in 1997 and closed in 2003, turning into an Asian restaurant. It was originally called the Noah's Ark, possibly a wry allusion to the regular flooding caused locally by a Fleet river very prone to bursting its banks. A few doors beyond the next junction, a pizza takeaway at **No.121** occupies the former shop of A J Williams, a Victorian barber at the cutting edge of hairdressing technology **[26]**.

We turn right, however, into busy **SWINTON STREET** and walk up its north side. It was built on land ('Acton Meadow') acquired from Henry Gough in 1776-78 by builder James Swinton and his brother Peter, a doctor. The street began as a short cul-de-sac off Gray's Inn Lane, its eastern extension being completed only in 1844. Three-storey houses remain at the eastern end of the north side. At **No.14** the art historian Sidney Charles Hutchison was born in 1912. In 1968 Hutchison became Secretary to the Royal Academy, a post he held until his retirement in 1982. He was known for his erudition, not least in his role of after-dinner speaker. Beyond the railway bridge, the northern side is now given over to the long brick-and-glass **Audiology Centre** of the late 1980s, and the **Nuffield Hearing & Speech Centre**, some two decades older, both associated with the nearby specialist hospital (p 88). The site behind them once contained Huskisson's chemical works, whose fumes must have blighted Victorian Swinton Street, much as the traffic of the King's Cross one-way system does today. On part of the old chemical works site, at No.78 was built shortly before WWI the Steel Smelters Hall, home of the Iron & Steel Trades Confederation, the metal workers' trade union. The hall was the venue for the meeting on the 20 and 21 April 1915 at which was formed the National Guilds League that later became part of the Communist Party.

On the south side, the original houses survive. The first date from the early 1840s; note their iron first-floor balconies and the Ionic imposts to their doors. Perched above the railway cutting is a Victorian factory at **No.27**, once the cab-building works of the London Improved Cab Co. (also p 76), and now primarily apartments.

From here, view the block past the turning on the south side ahead. It dates from the late 18th century. By the bus stop is **No.57**, which has a typically Georgian black-painted wooden doorcase with a broken pediment, and **Swinton's**, formerly the King's Head pub.

Now wait for a pause in the stream of traffic and cross over to walk along **SWINTON PLACE**, until 1937 Cross Street, a short roadway leading to **ACTON STREET**. Like its northerly neighbour, Acton Street began as a short cul-de-sac, laid out over Acton Meadow, the field that the Swinton brothers acquired. It was extended eastward between 1830 and 1849. Most of the original 3-storey houses survive, but **Nos.44-62** to your right were rebuilt in the 1990s. Look across the road to the left. **No.17** was the home of the actor Lionel Benjamin Rayner, where he died in 1855. He had built the Strand Theatre, initially naming it Rayner's New Subscription Theatre, but unable to obtain a licence had been obliged to close it after a few months. In 1850 the poet Harold Simmons died of cancer at his lodgings in **No.29,** his death hastened by the shock from an explosion that occurred while he was sailing up the Thames. The former Prince Albert pub – now a Konstam restaurant, obtaining all its ingredients from within the M25 – on the north side on the far corner with King's Cross Road is an ugly 1922 rebuild unworthy of a deviation. Instead, turn right and continue in the opposite direction to pass the **Queen's Head** (a young Victoria). Interestingly, this pub and the former King's Head in Swinton Street are identical in size and stand exactly back-to-back.

We soon reach the junction with **GRAY'S INN ROAD.** Glance south to where a few early (c.1777) houses survive in what was the start of Constitution Row. At No.2 a medical establishment was set up here at the start of 1802, much to the horror of the neighbours, who threatened litigation. The London Fever Hospital for infectious diseases (other than smallpox) had been founded the year before, and its 16-bedded House of Recovery provided for a time the main facility for fever patients for the whole of London. 170 were admitted in its second year, after which more than 60 patients were admitted annually. In 1816 it moved to a new building alongside the Smallpox Hospital to the north of the New Road, where it remained until 1848, when the Great Northern Railway required the land to build King's Cross station. With the compensation received, the hospital was rebuilt in Liverpool Road, Islington.

Constitution Row originally stretched north to what is now King's Cross Bridge, but its other buildings have gone. We turn right here past a series of unremarkable

modern blocks, including **Headland House**, whose name recalls the earlier occupation of the site by the farmworkers' union. It houses the National Union of Journalists. It covers the site of No.308, where the Independent Labour Party was resident from 1923-24. Beyond it is modern **Acorn House** (Terrence Higgins Trust). On this spot once stood No.8 Constitution Row, later No.314, where lived and died the engraver Joseph Collyer the younger (1748–1827). He engraved works by contemporary artists for the rich print seller Alderman Boydell and the ill-fated Shakespeare Gallery in Pall Mall. Collyer was appointed portrait engraver to Queen Charlotte, and was a member of the Stationers' Company, becoming Master in 1815. Another engraver, William Thomas Fry, lived from 1830 at No.9 (later No.316), also on the site of Acorn House.

Across Swinton Street the interwar, 7-storey block is called **Swinton House** (Nos.322-326). The doorway on the corner, still inscribed "Bank", belonged to a long-closed branch of the National Provincial, which supplanted a Victorian fourpenny doss house, which Booth in 1898 said was very rough. No.324 was in 1927 the address of the National Council of Labour Colleges, a Left-wing workers' education organisation, and of the *Sunday Worker* (1926). The occupiers of Swinton House included from 1942 to 1948 the Communist Party's newspaper the *Daily*

Worker, as a tenant of the Iron & Steel Trades Confederation. The newspaper was printed in a semi-detached part of the building, at No.74 Swinton Street, formerly belonging to Caledonian Press, printer of several Communist publications in the 1920s.

The **Water Rats** public house at **No.328** refers to its present owners, the Grand Order of Water Rats (the entertainers' charity). Its theatre, noted in the 1970s as old-time music hall, still offers a variety of evening entertainment. Until c.1990 the pub proudly bore the historic name of the Pindar of Wakefield (for the origin of the name, see p 105). That venerable tavern, patronised at different times by both Marx and Lenin, originally stood on the opposite side of the road south of Cromer Street, but was relocated here, the present building dating from 1878. Next door is the **Royal National Throat, Nose & Ear Hospital**, opened four years earlier with just ten beds as the *Central London* Throat, Nose & Ear Hospital, a new wing being added in 1906. It became part of the Royal Free Hospital Trust in 1996. Sharing the site is the Ear Institute Centre for Auditory Research of University College London.

Immediately beyond the Ear Institute Centre once stood St Jude's Church of 1862, designed by Joseph Peacock in a 'rogue gothic' style, and built in red and yellow brick. It was built to replace a temporary church erected in 1848, next to the National school in Britannia Street, which lies just to the east. The church closed in 1936, its parish uniting with that of Holy Cross (p 110); Gray's Inn Road, which once contained three churches, then had none. No explanation has been found for the unexpected Continental-style shutters at **Nos.334&336**, which is now offices of the neighbouring Institute, and was previously a commercial laundry.

North of Britannia Street is a site once occupied by the large premises of the Home & Colonial Schools Society, an Anglican institution founded in 1836 for the training of infant-school teachers along the lines of Pestalozzi. The pedagogical equivalent of a teaching hospital, it comprised four distinct 'model' schools, whose pupils paid upwards of 3d a week for the privilege of being 'practised' upon. It trained some 140 teachers a week, but by the end of the century the educational authorities declared the premises inadequate and the Society was given an ultimatum to leave. It moved out in 1903 to Wood Green, and a red-brick 4-storey Edwardian office building, later called Pioneer House, was constructed at **Nos.344-352**, extending through to Wicklow Street behind. This, for some 30 years, housed various departments of the London Co-operative Society, including the Co-operative Press, along with the headquarters of *Reynold's News*. Part of it is now occupied by offices of the MLS Business Centres and a Lloyds Bank.

Meanwhile, the west side is fronted by a continuous early-19th-century terrace (Nos.251-309) running between Argyle Street and St Chad's Street. South of King's Cross, Gray's Inn Lane bisected Battle Bridge Field, owned in 1710 by the De Beauvoirs of Hackney. The Field's eastern half, which we explored earlier, had already been built on by 1800. The rest had been divided up and sold to a number of different owners, including Messrs Robinson, Dunston and Flanders, who in 1824 sought an Act of Parliament to authorise building. Houses in Chichester Place, as the west side of Gray's Inn Road was known here, were among the first to be built. **No.291** is unique in not having a shop front at ground level, and has rusticated stucco and two timber sash windows.

In the centre of the terrace is **No.277**, once with an arch but now sporting a large green door. This was formerly the 'City Entrance' of the North London Horse & Carriage Repository (c.1827-28), an impressive classical structure built around a courtyard, with a lavishly appointed assembly room at one end and a mansion at the other **[27]**. North London's answer to Tattersall's, it offered high-class stabling and auction facilities, but apparently failed in this role, for the owner, William Bromley, had within two years transformed it into his Royal London Bazaar. In 1831 Robert Owen (p 98) helped establish here

an Institution of the Society to Remove the Cause of Poverty & Ignorance. The following year he opened his Equitable Labour Exchange, a short-lived co-operative enabling poor artisans to barter their skills for goods, using a currency based on the value of labour. Sharing the premises was Rev. Edward Irving, who came here with much of his congregation after his expulsion from Regent Square (p 108). Neither stayed long: Irving disliked being associated with Owen, who himself soon moved on (ejected, some say) after a dispute over rent. In 1833-35 Mme Marie Tussaud settled here with her waxworks after 26 years of touring. A "Second Room, inadvisable for ladies to visit", featuring death masks of murderers and guillotined French revolutionaries, was the forerunner of the Chamber of Horrors. After two seasons here Marie moved on to Baker Street, and the building was used for a furniture depository and then as a draughtsmen's office. As the 'Palace of Hygiene' it dispensed quack remedies; while as 'St George's Hall' the *piano nobile* played host to evangelists, panoramas and promenade concerts. In 1872 Whitbread's acquired the property, rebuilding it as a bottled beer store, which it remained until 1968. An elaborate Ionic portico, two storeys high, which had graced the Bazaar entrance was removed by the brewery to improve access.

Back on the east side, **King's Cross Travelodge** now occupies Willing House (c.1910). The building is an exuberant Tudor-Baroque assemblage designed by Hart & Waterhouse for the prosperous

oriel window, while adorning the arched entrance are symbols of the advertiser's role as communicator. Removed to Mayfair c.1970, Willing's had been established locally since Victorian times, operating as

storey buildings, one can just make out a large painted legend on the exposed end wall of **No.370**. From 1873 until c.1910 this was the hall of the non-sectarian London Cabmen's Mission, which initially incorporated a cabbies' shelter. *THANKFULLY RECEIVED WITHIN*, says the sign, no longer specifying what was requested, though it was probably money!

A much clearer painted sign remains visible on the façade of **Nos.319 & 321** opposite, recalling the presence here before WWII of Messrs Herbert & Co., makers of "scales, weights and weighing machines".

Gray's Inn Road now bends quite sharply to the west so that, in ancient times, it could cross the river at Battle Bridge to follow the east bank northward along the (then curving) line of Pancras Road. The first houses built on the right were known in the 18th century as White Hart Row, after the pub on the corner, and by the early 19th century as St Chad's Row. At No.20 St Chad's Row lived the engraver James Neagle (1765-1822), previously resident in Acton Street. He could expect at least 10 guineas (£10.50) a plate, and was once paid double that. No.23 was the home of the trumpeter Thomas Harper (1786–1853), inspector of musical

Willing's advertising agency. It was latterly the headquarters of the City and Guilds Examination Board, and is now Grade-II-Listed. A statue of Mercury stands atop a pyramidal roof, winged lions support a large

"showcard makers" at modest **No.366**, which still stands next door on the corner of St Chad's Place.

Across King's Cross Bridge, beyond a collection of rather ramshackle one-

27 The North London Horse & Carriage Repository, looking north towards the assembly rooms and Derby Street entrance (T H Shepherd, 1828)

instruments to the East India Company and principal trumpet at Drury Lane and at the Italian Opera. He played the slide trumpet throughout his life, making important contributions to its development, and wrote a tutor. His house and all the others in the row were demolished for the excavations of the Metropolitan Railway.

We soon regain the Lighthouse Building. After WWII **No.374** was the base of the International Brigade Association, which had sent the volunteer anti-fascist brigade to Spain during the Civil War. From 1955 until after 1970 it provided offices for the Movement for Colonial Freedom, long associated with the Leftist Fenner Brockway (p 17). Around 1968, it was also home to the British Campaign for Peace in Vietnam, then at the peak of its activity. Earlier, the adjacent **No.376** was the office in 1926-1930 of *The Worker*, the journal of the National Minority Movement, which had a pedigree dating back to the Red Clydeside strikes of 1916-19. Indeed, the vicinity of King's Cross was a stronghold of Left-wing politics. At various times it contained the headquarters of the Independent Labour Party (No.197 King's Cross Road, 1959-70); the Socialist Party of Great Britain (No.1A Caledonian Road, 1905-6, in Islington) and the Workers' International League, a relatively successful Trotskyite group (No.61 Northdown Street, 1940-44, also in Islington). The offices of *Workers' Life*, the predecessor of the *Daily Worker*,

were at No.29 Euston Road, 1927-29. But by far the most important site was St Pancras Town Hall (see p 100).

On the opposite side of Gray's Inn Road, the shop frontages fringe a site once occupied by an enormous, century-old, heap of dust and ashes, owned by one John Smith. (This dust heap was *not*, as is often supposed, the inspiration for the dust heap in *Our Mutual Friend*, as it had disappeared, see later, some decades before Dickens wrote in 1862 about dust heaps stretching *north-eastwards* from King's Cross to the Holloway Road.) There must have been organic refuse here too, for the tip was said to provide forage for 100 pigs. W Forrester Bray (p 103) purchased the dust heap for £500, having bargained it down from £800. It is often said that Bray sold 1,000 tons of the cinder heap to the Emperor of Russia for the rebuilding of Moscow after Napoleon's invasion, but this story has never been verified. The mound was finally removed only in 1826, and development of the western part of Battle Bridge field could proceed, but any hopes there may have been of raising the tone of the neighbourhood were thwarted by the presence of the Smallpox and Fever Hospitals, and the later advent of the two mainline termini. We shall see efforts to do so – for example the Panarmonion, Argyle Square (p 103) and Regent Square (p 108) in Route 10, which also starts from King's Cross.

The Skinners' estate and Euston Road
Circular walk from King's Cross
(see back cover for map)

Leaving King's Cross Underground station by the Euston Road (South Side) exit, walk west along the south side of Euston Road to a concrete-faced building, the newer part of Camden Town Hall. This is separated from its older part by a narrow footway, once the northern end of Tonbridge Street. Turn left into it, and then right along **BIDBOROUGH STREET**.

Bidborough is a village near Tonbridge (Kent), and the two names are an indication that we are entering the Skinners' estate, on which we shall see several Kentish towns and villages featuring in the street names. Sir Andrew Judd (d.1558) vested the land in the Skinners' Company, as trustees for the school he had founded at Tonbridge in response to the dissolution of the monasteries. The Skinners' Company then governed the use, production and sale of furs for trimming the garments of high-ranking people. Known as Sandhills (or Sandfield), the property extended westwards to Burton Street, as well as north-eastward onto the site of the future

ROUTE **9**

91

St Pancras station. From c.1807 building leases were granted to James Burton, who had already developed a large part of the Foundling estate to the south.

The east end of Bidborough Street was first known as Claremont Place. On the left is the **Dolphin** pub, one of several sites of which the livery company still owns the freehold, as shown by the small coat of arms high above the false door on the corner. The **Camden Centre**, formerly St Pancras Assembly Rooms, and part of the Town Hall block, faces the north side of **Queen Alexandra Mansions**, one of many blocks of red-brick mansion flats built in this area before WWI by the London Housing Society (LHS), a limited company that was still based in Judd Street until the late 1970s. The LHS was one of the web of companies and public utility societies initiated from about 1907 by Abraham Davis (a local ward councillor and future alderman), often in conjunction with one or other of his brothers. They promoted soundly-built flats in North London, notable examples being the lady workers' homes on the Holly Lodge Estate, Highgate.

A blue plaque recalls the residence here at Flat 176, from 1914 and intermittently for 22 years, of the war artist Paul Nash and his wife Margaret Theodosia. A neighbour of theirs in 1916 was the actress Mary Clare, leading lady in Noel Coward's *Cavalcade*. Ebenezer Landells,

wood engraver, illustrator, and magazine proprietor established his first proper workshop in Bidborough Street at former No.22 in the 1830s. There he devised a new magazine based on the French *Le Charivari*, and the first edition of *Punch, or the London Charivari*, in which Landells had a one-third share, appeared in 1841.

Avoiding the singularly charmless west end of the street, turn left into **JUDD STREET,** named after Sir Andrew Judd. Built in the early 19th century as a continuation of Hunter Street, its east side here is occupied by more LHS mansion flats and the **Skinners' Arms** pub, predating 1839. This is another Skinners' freehold. Diagonally opposite, at **No.123**, and once known as Kelvin House, is a British Telecom building dating from just before WWII, which served as the North Trunk (later International) Exchange. To its south is the headquarters of the **Royal National Institute for the Blind**, formerly occupied by the Salvation Army, latterly housing its Social Services Department and International Heritage Centre. The building opened in 1911 as the Army's publishing and supplies HQ. Here uniforms and bonnets were made, and from here musical instruments were despatched. Henry Hall, the future dance-band leader and radio broadcaster, was employed here at the age of 16 as a music copyist. His boss, Richard Slater, helped to develop his talents as both instrumentalist

and composer. Hall's *Sunshine March*, composed at this time, later became the basis for his BBC signature tune, *Here's To the Next Time*.

Continue along the street and note opposite the terrace (possibly by Burton) at **Nos.87-103**, some with old shop fronts, including the fine Corinthian specimen at **No.95**, a former butcher's. Nos.87-91 retain their original front doors. Now use the zebra crossing to reach **Medway Court** flats. Behind its railings a north-facing plaque celebrates the completion here in 1955 of the 2000th dwelling built by St Pancras Council since WWII. A Camden branch library occupied a unit on the ground floor until (now relocated) St Pancras Library opened at No.100 Euston Road in 1971. The flats cover the site of No.79, home to Theodore Lane, painter and etcher, who died here in 1828 after being injured at the horse repository in Gray's Inn Road when he struck his head on a skylight. His best known work, *The Enthusiast*, is in the Tate Collection. Also on this spot was No.67, where the chemist Alphonse René Le Mire de Normandy lived until 1860. He took out a British patent in 1839 for indelible inks and dyes, and in 1841 he patented a method of hardening soap made from what were known as 'soft goods' by the addition of sulphate of soda. He also invented an apparatus for distilling sea water to obtain drinking water, which was commonly used on board ship and which formed the subject of a patent granted in 1851 and a medal in 1862.

South of Leigh Street (p 95), **Nos.62-63** are two Burton 4-storey houses of 1808-11. The cherubic statuette above the doorway at **No.63** has no obvious significance. Now a patisserie, the premises were for generations a sweetshop. Beyond, a service ramp descends into what was once Hunter Place, long home to the local police station. The building over the ramp fronting onto Judd Street began as replacement headquarters for No.8 Police District. Later, as McNaghten House, it was a council-run hostel for the homeless. Now named the The Generator, and with an entrance in Compton Place (p 66), it is part of a private-sector international chain of hostels for more privileged young travellers.

Beyond, on the corner of Tavistock Place, the 'luxury apartments' now dubbed **Albany House** were once the Central London Ophthalmic Hospital, which moved here from Gray's Inn Road (p 78) in 1913. Note the foundation stone laid by the Duchess of Albany. When the hospital closed in 1948 it was converted to house the University's Institute of Ophthalmology (now sited next to Moorfields Hospital). This section of Judd Street began as part of Hunter Street (ahead, see p 67). Previously on this corner, at No.36 Hunter Street, stood a well-known academy run by the radical Baptist schoolmaster Jonathan Dawson and attended by

the brothers of Charles Dickens.

Cross by the lights to reach 1930s **Clare Court**, opposite. These flats lie behind grand gilded railings supporting coats of arms and the fatalistic motto *Quod Deus vult*, a last outpost of borderline Bloomsbury before it melts into vulgarian King's Cross. North of Clare Court is an open space known to bureaucrats as **Judd Street Open Space**, but to everyone else as Bramber Green, from the name of an adjacent block of flats. Saved from office development, it opened in 1954 on a plot of ground which had been a temporary home to the ever-moving King's Cross Coach Station. Notice the images of plane-tree leaves cut into the tops of the boundary railings.

Turn right along **CROMER STREET** (also p 110), whose western end lay on the Skinners' estate. On the north corner at No.120 is **One KX**, a community health and arts centre opened in June 2007 by Central YMCA with very 21st-century aspirations. It is home to a wide range of fitness courses, e.g. martial arts and dance, but is also the venue for the Y touring theatre company giving access to the arts, as well as a community café. The building previously housed the Tonbridge School Club, founded in 1882 jointly by the Kentish school and the Judd Foundation. It originally combined the functions of boys' club and mission hall, but the two functions were split when Holy Cross Church (p 110)

was opened. The present building dates from 1932, as noted on its foundation stone laid by the master of the livery company.

Just to the east is the early-19th-century incarnation of the **Boot** tavern. Before 1800 it was, as the Golden Boot, one of the few buildings in the area. On one map it was marked as the *Boat*-in-the-Fields. As well as liquor it offered a tea room and skittle alley, while adjoining it to the north and west were Bowling Green House and its two greens. Bowls was then often an excuse for the kind of rowdy behaviour for which this early leisure complex was infamous. In *Barnaby Rudge*, Dickens portrays the Boot as the headquarters of his fictional band of troublemakers in the 1780 Gordon Riots. Adjoining the pub is **Speedy Place**, a short (once longer) alley leading nowhere, its name commemorating a family whose tenure as landlords of the Boot spanned three centuries. It now houses the Tudor College, which looks out onto a green oasis of climbing plants, but was not always such a pleasant enclave. Its north end was marked dark blue and black on Booth's poverty map.

The roadway in front of the tavern once contained an ice house, and was known until 1867 as Greenland Place; nine houses had been built here as early as 1741. On Horwood's 1799 map of London they can be seen in the midst of fields alongside the bowling green. **Bramber** flats, opposite the pub, cover the site of Thomas Bryson's piano works at No.5; and of No.4, set back from the street and known fancifully as 'Nell Gywnne's Cottage' and as 'Compo Castle' because of its elaborate composition mouldings placed there by an early owner, nicknamed 'Compo Jack', adorned with Hebrew inscriptions and grotesque heads and surmounted by a lion passant. A Lion Terrace and a Waterloo Place once adjoined. Behind the house there once lay a cul-de-sac called Greenland Grove and later renamed Lucas Place. Compo Jack is most likely to have been the plasterer James Jonathan Hughes Delight Lucas. The family hailed from Norfolk, which may explain the name of Cromer Street, though the connection, if any, between James's family and Joseph Lucas, its original developer (see p 110) is unclear. James's two sons, Charles Thomas and Thomas, were born in Greenland Place in 1822 and 1826 respectively. Together they set up the public works company Lucas Brothers in 1844. Among their works was the Opera House and Floral Halls at Covent Garden; Charing Cross, Liverpool Street and Cannon Street stations; and the Royal Albert Hall. By 1870 the firm was one of the largest employers of labour in the country. Thomas was eventually knighted. As No.123 Cromer Street, their birthplace served various commercial purposes until 1938, when it was wantonly destroyed as part of an Air Raid Precautions exercise. The German bombs which fell nearby would probably have spared it!

Beyond the next left-hand corner are the flats of **Cromer House**. They cover the site of No.100, home until 1846 to Edward Williams (1781–1855), a member of a family of engravers who became a landscape painter. This area was then something of an artist's quarter. The Tate and various provincial museums hold examples of Williams' work.

Turn left into **TONBRIDGE STREET**, the eastern boundary of the Skinners' estate, where no original houses remain. The southern end was first called Joseph Street, after its developer Joseph Lucas. On the west side are **Tonbridge Houses**, a model dwellings block of 1904 built by the East End Dwellings Company (also p 111), whose sphere of operation extended outside the area suggested by its name. Peace Cottages, which previously stood on this site, were doubtless euphemistically (or apotropaically) named; Booth marked them dark-blue and black in 1898. Further north, on the corner of Argyle Walk is an Edwardian building that houses the Argyle drop-in centre, which provides family learning. It stands in the grounds of the **Argyle Primary School**, long named Manchester Street School after the street (p 105) in which its entrance was once located. Though opened by the London School Board in 1880, the building is misleadingly inscribed '1902', the date of its enlargement.

Turn left into **HASTINGS STREET**, a combination of pre-1840 Speldhurst Grove and Speldhurst Street, each named after another Kentish village. The latter was briefly home to the widowed Mary Shelley and her small son Percy soon after their return from Italy in 1823. Once again, nothing survives of the houses built by Burton and his contemporaries, and LHS mansion flats dominate the scene. The passenger lifts installed in **Hastings House** (left) in 1908-09 were described by the LCC as "somewhat novel for this class of dwelling". Facing the block is the south side of **Queen Alexandra Mansions**, where the comic actor Kenneth Williams spent three separate spells between 1959 and 1972, successively in Flats 66, 92 and 80.

Cross over busy Judd Street and soon turn left into **THANET STREET**, built as Lancaster Street and known as such until 1840. On the east side (left) reach a delightful row of half-stuccoed 2-storey workers' cottages, probably by Burton. The west side is lined by two more LHS blocks, **Thanet House** – note the cast-iron window guards in vine leaves with grapes – and **Rashleigh House**, which sandwich the modern **International Lutheran Students' Centre**, on the site of the National School of 1872 by William Milford Teulon, younger brother of Samuel Sanders. After the start of WWII the school was named Thanet Hall and put to various commercial uses until demolished in 1976.

At the end of Thanet Street, turn right into **LEIGH STREET**, built in 1810-13 by Burton and others and named after a village in Kent. Around 1850 Henry Mayhew, co-founder of *Punch* and author of *London Labour & the London Poor*, lived briefly with his wife and children at No.1 (at the western end) in 1850. On the largely intact south side, some attractive old shop fronts remain, along with a mixture of small shops and eating places which has long characterised the street. At No.8, now part of a fish restaurant, the landscape painter William Frederick Witherington lived from 1834 to 1847. He was elected to the Royal Academy, and exhibited there for over half a century. Several of his pictures are in Tate Britain and the Victoria and Albert Museum.

On the opposite side is the splendidly tiled **Norfolk Arms** in an ornate 'blood and bandages' building dated 1895, which replaced an earlier pub first licensed in 1826. It once had a smaller companion two doors away on the Thanet Street corner, the 'Suffolk Arms'; but that was a beer retailer's rather than a pub.

The pub turns the corner into **SANDWICH STREET**, up which we walk. Until 1840 it was called Hadlow Street, after a village near Tonbridge. A range of 4-storey houses similar to those in Leigh Street remains at **Nos.1-9**. The street was long a centre of services to the poor: a soup kitchen in 1848 was followed by a parochial library, and in 1873 by neo-Gothic St Pancras Mission Hall, designed by W M Teulon, with a school adjoining at the rear. After WWII, the hall was let, and later sold, to the Lutherans. **St Mary's with St George's German Lutheran Church** was founded as St Mary's off the Strand in 1694 as the church of St Mary-le-Savoy. Its c.1976 rebuild, here on the mission hall site, is below ground, with a student hostel above.

Passing **Sandwich** and **Sinclair Houses** (right), turn left along Hastings Street. On the tall tower block on the south side note the plaque recording the site of the Plumber's Arms public house, here from c.1808 to 1972. At the junction ahead pause to look north along **MABLEDON PLACE**, where the sole surviving house, little **No.12**, was once the Sandhills estate office. The rebuilt pub now called **Mabel's** was the Kentish Arms until 1968, when it became the Escape, displaying memorabilia of WWII prisoners of war. **No.1**, the tall concrete tower of UNISON, the major public service trade union, was built c.1976 for NALGO, one of its constituent parts. Mabledon Place was widened in 1902, at the same time losing a protective bar gate at the north end. In 1850 this corner hit the headlines, when a stag, pursued from Hendon by the huntsmen and hounds of one Mr Bean, negotiated the streets of Somers Town, crossed the New Road and, terrified by the traffic (even then!), leapt over the Mabledon Place bar to seek sanctuary in an ironmonger's shop **[28]**.

On the east side of the Place is **Hamilton House** (1913), headquarters of the National Union of Teachers. On this site, at No.19, the poet Shelley stayed on business in 1817, visited alternately by wife Mary, then seeking a publisher for her *Frankenstein*, and his stepsister-in-law Claire Clairmont. To its north is **Bidborough House**, an undistinguished 1960s office block containing Camden's Housing Department. Here once stood the factory of Messrs Voile & Wortley, listed in 1859 as dry-salters, but a century later as makers of liquorice. The site had been occupied in 1818-30 by a riding school, and later by livery stables. The horse statue that once graced Voile's premises now stands in the inner courtyard of the modern block.

Mabledon Place was popular with wood engravers, notably John Orrin Smith, a principal engraver for the newly established *Illustrated London News*. He died in 1843 at No.11 from 'apoplexy' brought on by the shock of a shower bath. The Williams family of engravers lived in the neighbourhood in the 1830s. The work *Sancho Requesting the Duchess to Superscribe his Letter* was undertaken at No.5. Helena Wells Whitford, novelist and educationalist, died in the street in 1824. She advocated the establishment in

28 Mabledon Place bar, 12 Feb 1850: Mr Bean's stag hunt comes to town (Heal Collection)

Yorkshire of a type of Protestant nunnery, which she envisaged as a national house of refuge for respectable females who needed help, either to equip them for a teaching career or to shelter them in old age.

Turning south, we are now in **CARTWRIGHT GARDENS**, built by James Burton in 1809-20, and known as Burton Crescent until 1908. That year the crescent was renamed after former resident John Cartwright, once a naval man, later a major in the Territorial Army. Known as the 'Father of Reform', he campaigned for universal male suffrage, annual parliaments and against slavery, and was the first English author openly to support American independence. A bronze statue in his honour, unveiled in 1831, sits in the central gardens, now given over to tennis courts for use by residents. The crescent's change of name may have been prompted by the stigma attached to it by two horrible murders, including the unsolved 'Burton Crescent Murder' of 1878, when Rachel Samuel, an elderly widow, was battered to death at No.4. A female former servant of hers was charged with the offence, but was acquitted for lack of evidence. *The Cartwright Gardens Murder* (1924), a long-forgotten detective novel by J S Fletcher, concerns a wholly unrelated fictitious case of poisoning, set here in what it described as a "drab and dismal crescent". *Cartwright Gardens* is the title of a poem (1995) by Jacques Roubaud, the French mathematician and experimental poet.

Walk south along the crescent's eastern chord, which was damaged in WWII and is now lined by London University's three 'Garden Halls' of residence built progressively over two decades, on a long lease from the Skinners. These are **Hughes Parry Hall** (which includes the tall tower block we just passed), **Canterbury Hall** (with winged cherubs above the entrance) and **Commonwealth Hall**. The houses at Nos.1-6 on the site of the last had latterly been converted into the Brighton Hall Restaurant. A brown plaque commemorates the residence in 1837-9 at erstwhile No.2 of Rowland Hill, the former teacher whose 1837 pamphlet on Post-Office Reform led to the establishment of the Penny Post two years later. No.2 was also home to Dr David Cooper (1817-42), the naturalist and author of *Flora Metropolitana*. The Scottish novelist John Galt lived at No.9 in 1813-14; No.10 was home in 1841-44 to the eccentric church architect Edward Buckton Lamb; and No.18 is thought to have been a London pied-à-terre of William Moon, remembered for his system of embossed print for the blind. Golding Bird, the physician, was apprenticed to an apothecary in Burton Crescent in 1833. Later, he was put in charge of the new electrical treatment room at Guy's, where he investigated the value of shock treatment to relieve paralysed limbs and the action of electricity on the nervous system.

Burton's two western quadrants survive intact, though much altered. The southwest curve, along which we turn, appeared, surprisingly, on Booth's poverty map in deep blue (for very poor), reflecting the presence at **No.45** of the Society for the Rescue of Young Women & Children, and at **No.49** of the Main Memorial Home for Deserted Mothers. James White, author and advertising agent, died at **No.47** in 1820. He had romantic ideas about the feasting practised in 'Old' England, and organised May Day feasts for London's chimney sweeps, as related by Charles Lamb in one of his essays. He served sausages instead of beef and pudding, acting as head waiter himself.

The North London Deaconesses' Institution was housed at **No.50,** founded by Elizabeth Catherine Ferard (1825-83), who became the first Church of England deaconess, and by Rev. Thomas Dale, vicar of St Pancras, a relation by marriage. The institution was a residential society of ladies for charitable work for the poor and for nursing, but required no vows. Ferard became the head sister. **Nos.51-53** were a YMCA hostel in 1920, but since before WWII this quadrant has been occupied by small hotels. View from here the northwest curve, which is lined by **Cartwright University Halls** (formerly Bentham Hall, acquired by UCL in 1932), including **Nos.31-33**, home in WWII to the Club for

Educated Women Workers, later the Club for Students & Professional Women. These were being renovated in early 2008. **No.36** was home in 1859 to the wood engraver Matthew Sears. John Cartwright (see above) lived at **No.37** from 1820 until his death 4 years later.

Turn left along short **BURTON PLACE**, originally Crescent Place, where Robert Owen lived in the 1830s at No.4, a house adjoining, at the rear, a major hub of his many activities (see later). On the south side today is **Virginia Court,** a convincing 1994 pastiche which has, like **No.5** opposite, an imposing portico modelled on a surviving original at the opposite end of the Place. Behind is **Woolf Mews**, a contemporary development in what was once Crescent Mews South. (The Woolfs, incidentally, lived not here, but in Tavistock Square, a little to the west.)

Pause at the junction with **BURTON STREET,** which was developed in 1809-20 by the eponymous builder. Though under threat of demolition in 1973, the houses at the south end have been spared and restored, preserving the attractive (if mass-produced) trelliswork of their individual balconies. Most have four storeys, and would have been classified as 'first-rate' had they not been so narrow. Mary Matilda Betham, writer and self-taught miniature painter, died at **No.36** (left) in 1852. Family circumstances and poverty affected her mental health, and in 1819 she was confined as insane. She complained that her unconventionality made her family wish to keep her out of the way, but she did eventually retire to the country and relinquish her literary pursuits. When, as an elderly woman, she once more settled in London, her wit and stores of apt quotation and anecdote made her a favourite among literary people. On the west side, **Nos.14-16** rise to only two storeys, possibly because the money ran out. Burton often sublet leases to other builders, and breaks in brickwork here point to the houses' separate construction. At the far south end of the street once stood No.17, a substantial villa in its own grounds, which was home to John Britton, cellarman turned topographer and antiquary, who died here in 1857. His *The Beauties of England and Wales* ran to 27 bound volumes and took twenty years to complete; he wrote several hundred volumes on similar subjects. No.17 later housed the Burton House Collegiate School (previously in Regent Square). Latterly occupied by an ugly British Rail garage, the site is now covered by the sympathetically-styled housing association flats of **Leonard Court** (c.1994).

Burton Street was once a cul-de-sac at both ends, which explains its curious numbering scheme, starting in the middle opposite Burton Place, and running anticlockwise along the SW, E and NW sides to where it began. There was once a gate here giving access to old Tavistock House, which Burton had built as his own home. Later the site was taken up by three buildings – Russell, Bedford and Tavistock Houses, the latter the residence of James Perry, the editor of the *Morning Chronicle* for some years until he sold it to Charles Dickens in 1851, shortly before *Bleak House* was begun. Dickens held many amateur dramatic activities here before he sold the house for 2,000 guineas in 1860. At nearby No.4 lived the writer's first biographer, John Forster, who kept up the house, in his own words, as a "liberty hall". The old houses were demolished in 1901 and replaced by the present Tavistock House designed by Lutyens. The rear of this building now lines the north-west side of the street. Watercolourist George Sidney Shepherd died on the site in 1858 at No.47. At former No.49, James Pierrepont Greaves, the mystic, gathered a group of disciples at his home in Burton Street into an 'aesthetic institution'. They included literary men like F F Barham, who notoriously described Greaves as "essentially a superior man to Coleridge". Greaves died in 1842.

A rainbow of faiths made use of the Burton Street Hall (demolished 1927), whose site is marked by the 20th-century infill at **No.39**, to which we continue, right, passing the second-hand bookshop Marchmont Books. The Hall was built for the Particular Baptists in 1811 and later used by the reformer Robert Owen (p 89). The London Co-operative Society held its inaugural meeting here in 1824, before installing itself in Red Lion Square, and Owen continued to use the hall for his 'social festivals' (or lectures) until 1837. Thereafter it was used by the Swedenborgians and, from 1849, as the St Pancras Free Church, which was not a nonconformist establishment but an offshoot of the nearby parish church, providing 275 free seats for the poor. Later still the hall became St Mary's RC school, then a Salvation Army citadel. No.39 is now called Tiger House, and comprises modern duplex studios built behind the original Burton terrace at Nos.40-45. James Malcolm Rymer, living at **No.42** in 1841 and acting as a civil engineer and inventor of an improved furniture caster, became a prolific novelist under the pseudonyms M J Errym and Malcolm J Merry. **No.45,** home to the Maghreb bookshop founded in 1987, is flanked by another entrance to Tiger House.

The roadway linking Burton Street with Duke's Road (to the north) did not exist before 1906. A flight of steps led down into what had been Draper's Place, described in 1860 as a vile slum where "squalor, disease and death were rampant with immorality and crime", and where typhus and gaol fever were rife. Renaming it Brantome Place in 1885, seemingly after a picturesque town in the Dordogne,

led to little improvement. Booth noted in 1898 a common lodging house for women "of disorderly character". The deputy who accompanied him was abused by two women "with a very choice selection from their vocabulary". Brantome Place was swept away, along with adjacent Crescent Mews North, and No.51 Burton Street also disappeared. The West London Synagogue of British Jews had been founded here in 1842. Six years later it moved to Margaret Street, Cavendish Square.

The demolition made space for the building by St Pancras Council of **FLAXMAN TERRACE** (1907-8), named after the Fitzrovia-based sculptor John Flaxman (d.1826). Designed by Joseph & Smithern, red-brick **Flaxman Court** is topped by two copper cupolas, exuding the civic pride of the day. Set repeatedly in the railings, though barely discernible through successive layers of paint, is the Council's badge depicting the boy martyr Pancratius. Opposite is an annexe of The Place (see below), housing the Contemporary Dance Trust, and standing on the site of the Victorian piano factory of Eavestaff & Sons. **Flaxman House** (at **No.1**) is an unusually grand caretakers' lodge, with its own pair of cupolas; it has now been redeveloped into residences.

DUKE'S ROAD, along which we continue north, dates from the 1760s, and was known as Duke's Row in the Georgian period. It stood on the boundary of the

Fitzroys' Tottenhall estate, hence the name of **Grafton Mansions** (1890) on the east side, the Duke of Grafton being head of the Fitzroy family. The road, however, takes its name from another peer, the 4th Duke of Bedford, who vigorously opposed the building of the New Road but eventually realised its benefits and upgraded a trackway running north out of his Bloomsbury estate to serve as his own private road to it. **Nos.2-16** on the west side form a fine terrace of former shops, an extension at right angles of Woburn Walk, Thomas Cubitt's delightful shopping parade of 1822, originally Woburn Buildings. They are now stuccoed and used mainly as offices, their smart black shop fronts redundant. **No.22**, on the south-east corner, now offices, was until the early 1930s the butterscotch factory of Messrs Callard & Bowser. Here previously lay a short cul-de-sac of 12 working-class houses, named Vittoria Place, presumably after the decisive battle of the Peninsular War.

The edifice we know as **The Place** was opened by the Prince and Princess of Wales in 1889 as the drill hall of what was later named The Artists' Rifles, TA, as can be seen by the elaborate terracotta decoration above the entrance. Its early volunteers included Millais, Holman Hunt, William Morris, and Robert Edis, the building's architect. Its site was earlier occupied, from 1846, by the Lord Nelson Music Hall, also known as the Euston

Music Hall, the New Music Hall and Frampton's. The drill hall is now home to a dance school, and the Place Theatre is London's foremost modern dance venue. The council flats named **Somerton House** take their name, tangentially, from Somer*set* Terrace, a former tributary of Duke's Road, whose site they occupy. Here, from c.1895, the suffragette Emmeline Pethick(-Lawrence) shared a mansion flat at No.20 with her friend Mary Neal, who helped revive traditional Morris dancing. The poor sewing-girls recruited to their Somers Town Esperance Club would rehearse their Morris routines on the flat roof of the block.

Continue past the back of St Pancras New Church, with a close-up view of its two groups of caryatids. For weary walkers, nearby Euston station (over to the left) now provides an escape route. Otherwise, cross **EUSTON ROAD** and walk east towards King's Cross along its north side, for a better view of the south side which concerns us here. South Row and Stones Row, the stretch of the New Road east of Duke's Road, were first developed in the 1790s in a corner of Lord Somers' estate, and so were, strictly, part of Somers Town. The 1756 Act of Parliament which authorised the construction of the New Road stipulated that no new buildings be erected within 50 feet of the carriageway, so as not to impede troop movements. The terraces of large houses which at first lined the road therefore had long front gardens. In the 19th century many of the gardens were acquired by monumental masons, who filled them with their statuary. Here in South Row was a colony of funerary specialists, including a mason's, a marble works, and factories making coffins, wreaths and crosses. Penetrating this small industrial enclave was Inwood Place, named after the locally based family of architects, responsible for St Pancras New Church. Blitzed in WWII, the site of Inwood Place is now covered by a 1960s block of offices and council flats and the **Premier Travel Inn,** decorated in lilac and battleship grey.

Beyond Mabledon Place the red-brick offices of 1930s **Clifton House** – now with prominent entrances marked No.101 – and the **Euston Flyer** pub (1998) cover a site earlier used briefly in the 1930s for a 'Euston Market' before being replaced by a car showroom. Local people remember it with some affection, recalling a shop in which two live bears were kept that later moved to Judd Street, and a stall that sold sheet music at 6d a sheet. This stretch of the New Road was called Tonbridge Place. At No.3 died William Prowse CB (1752-1826), naval officer, who took part in the Battle of Trafalgar and was eventually promoted to rear-admiral. The once gloomy 1950s railway offices of Great Northern House have been cheerfully refurbished as the **St Pancras International Youth Hostel** (Nos.79-81). This stands on the site of the Euston Cinema, damaged beyond repair in WWII, which was in turn built on the site of the Congregational Tonbridge Chapel (founded 1810); a century later it served as the Christian Catholic Church in Zion, an American evangelistic establishment.

At the junction with Judd Street is the erstwhile Euston Tavern. Rebuilt after wartime damage, it became **O'Neill's** Irish theme pub in 1996. On the corner beyond is **Camden** (formerly St Pancras) **Town Hall**. It was opened in 1937, replacing the Vestry Hall near St Pancras Old Church. Steel-framed, faced in Portland stone, and roofed in Westmorland slate, it was dismissed by Pevsner as "unremarkable neo-Palladian". The town hall was the scene of major disruption on May Day 1958 when the Red Flag was joyfully raised by Labour Councillor John Lawrence, a sometime Trotskyist. It subsequently became the venue for Communist Party of Great Britain conferences from 1959 to 1981. The site was called Hamilton Place in the early 19th century; the architect E B Lamb lived here in 1828-9. Later, the houses were colonised by offices of coal merchants and colliery agents, whose trade flourished in the railway lands to the

29   A funfair complete with rollercoaster occupies the site of the future Camden Town Hall [c.1931]

north. They were demolished in the mid-1920s, after which the vacant site was used temporarily for a small funfair, complete with a 'figure of eight' rollercoaster [29].

The 8-storey **Town Hall Extension**, designed by the Council's own architects, sprouted on the Argyle Street corner in 1977-8. **St Pancras Library**, greatly reduced in size, moved into the ground floor in 1993, on vacating its 22-year-old purpose-built

30   The so-called 'British College of Health' on the site of the present Camden Town Hall Extension

home at No.100 Euston Road. The unloved, unlovely modern block stands on the site of a much-loved theatre, opened at Nos.37-43

in 1900 as the Euston Palace of Varieties. Here Marie Lloyd performed, and actress Kay Hammond made her 1927 debut in *Tilly of Bloomsbury*, a romantic comedy by Ian Hay. Successively renamed Euston Theatre, Euston Music Hall, and Regent Theatre, it became a cinema in 1932, later renamed the Century, then the ABC, before closing as the Granada in 1968, to end its days as a bingo hall. No.33, on the corner site, was occupied until WWII by a Red Shield hostel of the Salvation Army, earlier by a temperance hotel, and before WWI by the pretentiously named British College of Health [30]. This was actually the research and manufacturing base of the firm founded by James Morison (d.1840), creator of the once world-famous Morison Vegetable Pill. A genuine medical establishment, the British Hospital for Diseases of the Skin existed in 1906 at No.29, where Barclays Bank now stands on the corner of Belgrove Street (p 103).

Back at King's Cross, stand in front of the mainline station and look over to the south side of Euston Road, where **No.1** was, from 1897 until the 1960s, the elegant Reggiori's restaurant, a Swiss-Italian establishment much admired for the stained glass of its 'cathedral' windows and extravagant interior décor ([35], p 114). Notice how the original houses here were set back from the road to respect the 50-ft rule and how their gardens were later covered by single-storey shops.

South of King's Cross

Circular walk from King's Cross
(see back cover for map)

Of the two Euston Road (South Side) exits from King's Cross Underground station, take the one on the left and emerge up the flight of steps at the corner of **CRESTFIELD STREET**. This was begun, as Chesterfield Street, in 1825, even before the removal of Mr Smith's dust heap (p 91). It was one of several short streets named until 1937 after prominent peers of the realm or their seats, and built by William Forrester Bray on the site of the New Road nursery garden. Walk a few yards along the street and pause. On the east side is the plain brick post-WWII incarnation of **King's Cross Methodist Church** (p 113). South of it is a row of original houses. **No.5**, with a fine ironwork balcony, was the birthplace in 1851 of Edward Walter Maunder, astronomer. His study of the dearth of sunspots in the 16th century became known as the Maunder Minimum. The painter Charles Ginner (1878-1952) moved into **No.3**, now part of a hotel, in 1911, the year in which the Camden Town Group, of which he was a member, was formed.

Return to Euston Road, turn left and by the Post Office on the corner again left, along **BELGROVE STREET**. This is another of Bray's creations, the west side lined by some of the small private hotels which have characterised the Battle Bridge estate since the late 19th century, traditionally providing workspace for prostitutes, and earning King's Cross its perennial, now only historical, reputation as one of London's 'red light' districts. These former houses (Bray originals) were praised by the LCC Survey of London for their "admirable execution" and "ingenuity of design". In stark contrast, the east side is wholly dominated by the ugly brick premises behind 1930s **Belgrove House**. Home at first to the King's Cross Coach Station, they might have become a cinema, but instead served later as a GPO garage and sorting office, and are now a storage warehouse.

Continue along the west side of **ARGYLE SQUARE**, built after 1832 on part of the site of the projected Royal London Panarmonion. This grandiose scheme was to have occupied all of the area now contained by Argyle, Birkenhead and St Chad's Streets. Probably the brainchild of Gesualdo Lanza (1779-1859), an Italian music teacher and singing tutor who had a music-selling business in Chesterfield Street, it was meant to include a music academy, a large theatre flanked by ballroom and refreshment rooms, a gallery and hotel, reading and billiard rooms, and a botanical bazaar, all set in pleasure gardens, with the added attraction of a 'suspension railway', which was a sort of monorail, with a person-powered boat-shaped carriage **[31]**. The architect was Stephen Geary (p 82), better known for his design of Highgate Cemetery. The project was a complete flop, and its promoters faced bankruptcy. Although the gardens were laid out, the buildings were barely started, and the little that was built was demolished and auctioned off in 1832, to be replaced by houses with characteristic round-arched doorways and ground-floor windows, some partly stuccoed.

On Booth's poverty map the square appears as a splash of middle-class red, and census returns confirm a high proportion of artists and professionals. By 1900 the square was largely given over to private hotels, as it still is. For many years seedy, they are now considerably smarter. The neighbourhood's move up-market owes much to the refurbishment of **Argyle Square Gardens**, and their re-enclosure with railings to deter vagrants.

The houses on the north side of the square gave way to the building that is now the storage warehouse. At erstwhile No.2 lived Francis Oliver Finch (1802-62), the watercolour painter. Examples of his work are in the British Museum, the Victoria and Albert Museum, and the Yale Center for British Art. Michael Henry, patent agent turned newspaper editor and assistant editor of *The Jewish Chronicle*, died in 1875

SUSPENSION RAIL-WAY, ROYAL PANARMONION GARDENS,
LIVERPOOL STREET, KING'S CROSS, NEW ROAD, St. PANCRAS.

WILLIAM THE FOURTH, ROYAL CAR.

This astonishing Machine, now exhibiting in the Royal Panarmonion Gardens, is perhaps one of the most simple pieces of **Machinery** ever discovered, possessing such wonderful action, that many tons weight may be conveyed to any distance, without the help of steam or animal power. No one can believe that this Car travels with such ease and rapidity without being a witness of the fact. The idea is a very ingenious one, and does great credit to Mr. H. THORRINGTON who is the inventor. The admittance to the Gardens is One Shilling each Person, entitling **the parties to ride round the gardens in the Car, or on the Hobby Horse.** Refreshments may be obtained on the Premises.

104

at his home at former No.6, his clothing having been ignited by a candle flame while at his office in Fleet Street the previous day. In his memory, the Jewish Scholars' Life Boat Fund was founded and its first vessel was named the *Michael Henry*.

The east and west sides of the square are almost intact. Over on the east side, the French poet Arthur Rimbaud stayed in 1874, the year after his break with Verlaine, in a small hotel at **No.12**, awaiting the arrival of his mother and little sister Vitalie in London for sight-seeing and window-shopping. Here on the west side, at **No.46**, Walter Crane, chiefly remembered as a children's book illustrator, but then aged 17 and an engraver's apprentice, was living with his widowed mother in 1862. Reach the south side of the square. To our right is L-shaped Argyle Street. It continues beyond the south-east corner of the square, to which we now walk by turning left. This corner was destroyed in WWII, taking with it the New Jerusalem Church (see **[32]**, p 106). Built for the Swedenborgians in 1844, it was in neo-Norman style, in white and yellow brick, with twin 70-ft spires. Unassuming **No.30** nearby on this south side was once the Salvation Army's Prison Gate House, a hostel for discharged prisoners.

31   The monorail at the ill-fated Royal Panarmonion may have been erected and tested, but probably never carried passengers

Continue ahead along the eastern arm of **ARGYLE STREET**. This section was begun, as Manchester Street, in 1826, but not completed for another 14 years. No.51 on the left is the **King's Cross Neighbourhood Centre**. The garden alongside was the site of the mid-19th century Argyle Railway & Family Hotel **[32]** which survived until WWII. This stood on the corner of Liverpool Street, the line of which can be seen by looking through the gates of **Fleetfield** flats.

These face the flats of **Bedefield**, whose name recalls the de Bedefields, 14th-century landowners in the Lay Manor of St Pancras. Parallel to this block is **Gatesden**, named after John de Gatesden, lord of the manor in 1247. On this site stood No.18 Manchester Street, where the organ builder Henry Willis had the second of his several London workshops in the 1850s. It was here that he achieved his well-deserved fame by building the instrument for the Great Exhibition of 1851, which was later moved to Winchester Cathedral. He also built the organs for the Royal Albert Hall and St Paul's Cathedral. Beyond Gatesden are early-19th-century houses at **Nos.106-110**.

At **GRAY'S INN ROAD** turn right (south), passing the 19th-century **Lucas Arms** at the end of Cromer (once Lucas) Street and, beyond at **Nos.235-243**, the site of the ancient Pindar of Wakefield tavern. This was named not after the ancient Greek poet

but after a legendary Yorkshire folk hero, a contemporary of Robin Hood, and a bane of King John's tax collectors. A pinder was one responsible for penfolding or impounding stray cattle. Recorded in 1575 as being the only hostelry between Holborn and Highgate, it was destroyed by a 'hurricane' in 1724, and the landlord's two daughters were buried in the rubble. It was later rebuilt on the east side of the road at No.328 (p 88). **Nos.233-241**, an unmarked brick building of the late 1930s, once served as TERminus telephone exchange, and the metal frames of its huge windows are adorned by flaming torches and a series of stylised early handsets enclosed in wreaths.

Turn right into **HARRISON STREET**, built in a meadow called Peperfield, acquired in 1783 by Thomas Harrison, described as a farmer, though his family had by then been brickmaking for 160 years. The development of the Foundling estate to the south persuaded them that more money could be made from houses than from bricks. Nothing remains of the old street, where Paul Storr, gold- and silversmith to the royal family, working to designs by Flaxman, opened workshops at No.17 in 1819. William Thomas Fry, engraver, died at former No.41 and the Williams family of engravers, who flourished in the first three quarters of the 19th century, were also residents. Post-WWII blocks of council housing

106

now line most of both sides of the street. The six tall blocks on the right we shall describe on reaching Cromer Street (p 93). The rebuilt **Harrison Arms** stands on the corner of **SEAFORD STREET** (Francis Street till 1865), a short, now wholly 20th-century street, which we follow southward. South of the pub, from 1826 to 1904, stood a steam-engineering works run by successive generations of the extraordinarily inventive Perkins family – Jacob (of steam-gun fame, see p 20); his son Angier March Perkins (p 109), and his grandson Loftus. Here they made or developed a wide range of products exploiting the potential of high-pressure steam, from central-heating systems and commercial baking ovens to steam road vehicles and engines for ships. The premises later served as the button factory of Messrs Walmsley & Co., who survived WWII to become makers of board game components.

Pause on reaching **SIDMOUTH STREET**. Built by the Harrisons in 1807-18, though planned as early as 1799, this took its

32 'The proposed Argyle Railway & Family Hotel'; on the left, the Swedenborgians' New Jerusalem Church, destroyed in WWII

33 St Peter's Church (Regent Square) in 1828, consecrated 2 years earlier, but still set amidst the Harrison brickfields (from the *Gentlemen's Magazine*)

name from Lord Sidmouth, prime minister (1801-04) and Foundling Hospital vice-president (1802-44). To your left, on the north side today, is the post-WWII **Sidmouth Mews** development of low-rise council-flat blocks, comprising **Linfield**, **Tangmere** and **Warnham**. Many local blocks have Sussex place-names as they lay in the 'Sussex' zone of St Pancras Council's block-naming master plan. On the south side, erstwhile No.25 was the family home in 1840-43 of James William Hudson, a pioneer of adult education. By coincidence, its site is now covered by the 'King's Cross Centre' of **Westminster Kingsway College**, latter-day providers of such enlightenment. The eastern part of this campus was being demolished at the time of writing. Opened in 1958, the building initially housed the LCC's Starcross Upper School, a good mile south-east of its parent establishment near Euston station. The site was previously occupied by the Prospect Terrace Board Schools (1882) and public baths, devastated in wartime bombing. These in turn had supplanted Georgian Wellington Square, with its Prince Regent tavern, and the slums of diminutive Derry Street. Diagonally bisecting the site was Prospect Terrace, long the main entrance driveway to the burial grounds which became part of St George's Gardens (p 66). Now turn right along Sidmouth Street, whose only remaining houses, at Nos.51-55 on the left, have unusually

narrow first-floor windows. Matilda Maria Evans, social reformer, in her widowhood lived with her mother at **No.53**. "Bates's salve cures wounds and sores", boasts an old painted inscription on the end wall of **No.55**, the base before WWII of Messrs Bates & Co., makers of magnesium citrate.

Reach **REGENT SQUARE** and find a bench in the gardens. When the first houses appeared in Gravel Pit Field in 1829, George IV had become king, but the square had been planned and named by the Harrisons years before, under the Regency. The first buildings were the two elegant churches in contrasting styles which were to be the square's glory until WWII. On the east side was Anglican St Peter's, designed by William Inwood and his son Henry, the architects of St Pancras New Church, in a similar Greek Revival style, with a two-stage tower and a hexastyle Ionic porch **[33]**. Begun in 1822, it was consecrated 4 years later and flourished until WWII, when it suffered a direct hit. The portico survived till 1967, when despite vigorous protests it suffered a fate similar to that of Euston Arch. Occupying the church site today are the modern flats of **St Peter's House** and **St Peter's Court**.

In the south-west corner of the square was a Presbyterian chapel, whose congregation moved here from Hatton Garden. Known as the National Scotch (or Caledonian) Church, it was designed by Sir William Tite in a Decorated gothic

style, intended as a miniature version of York Minster **[34]**. Thomas Carlyle was at the stone-laying, and both Coleridge and Robert Peel were at the triumphal opening in May 1827. The congregation adhered to the Church of Scotland until the Disruption of 1843, when it joined the English Presbyterians. Its most famous minister in 1822-32 was the Rev. Edward Irving, whose theological views and unorthodox style of worship, which encouraged 'speaking in tongues', eventually led to his expulsion by the church authorities for heresy. He and 800 of his followers subsequently took refuge at the Royal London Bazaar (p 89). John Bate Cardale (1802-77), first apostle of the Catholic Apostolic Church, attended the Caledonian Church. Damaged "beyond repair" in a V2 attack in 1944, the gothic structure was demolished and replaced by the plain brick **Regent Square United Reformed Church**, currently being refurbished. Church House, the national headquarters of the URC is next door, at No.86 Tavistock Place.

A terrace of old houses survives on the south side of the square, where **No.6** was home for some 17 years to artist William Coldstream, a co-founder with Victor Pasmore (p 27) of the Euston Road School. **Nos.4-6** from c.1863-1904 were the Homes of Hope, for young women deemed too good for the workhouse but who needed to be saved from prostitution because of their previous good character;

by 1919 the houses had become a base of the Women's Training Corps. Isaac Seabrook, the builder of both the Inwood churches, lived at **No.1** and No.27 1832-1844. Iron lampposts erected by St Pancras Borough are still in use on this side of the square, fitted with modern replicas of Victorian lighting.

Council flats line the other three sides of the once war-ravaged square. On the north side, now taken up with the flats of **Rodmell**, (at No.36) lived James Strachey, brother of Lytton, and translator of Freud. Vanessa Bell listed him as an original member of the Bloomsbury Group, an association he always denied. On the west side, where **Storrington** now stands, No.18 was home in 1848-50 to Angier March Perkins, the celebrated American-born steam engineer. The actor William Henry Hartnell (1908-75), the original *Dr Who*, was born at No.24. Aldous Huxley lived briefly in 1921 at No.26 while his wife and baby were abroad, Huxley having recently become a journalist for *House and Garden*.

Regent Square Gardens gained notoriety in 1917 when the dismembered body of a woman was found here wrapped in brown paper. Louis Voisin, a Belgian butcher, had murdered an ex-lover at a

34   York Minster in miniature: the National Scotch Church, Regent Square (1829 etching, after a painting by T H Shepherd)

house in Fitzrovia, and made use of his vocational skills to dispose of the corpse. The gardens are better noted for their rather too lofty plane trees, whose height threatens their survival. Leaving the square in the north-west corner, follow a pleasantly landscaped footway northward to regain Harrison Street beside the tall block **Glynde Reach**.

Continue ahead to emerge into **CROMER STREET**, alongside **Holy Cross Church**, where we pause. Financed partly through the generosity of the Goodenoughs (p 56), this was dedicated in 1888. It replaced a mission hall opened 12 years earlier in what is now Argyle Walk. Towerless, and with a plain and undistinguished exterior, it was designed by Joseph Peacock, also architect of neighbouring St Jude's (p 88), from which some fittings were brought when the parishes merged in 1936. The church was always regarded as High Anglican, and in 1996 one mass each week was celebrated by a Roman Catholic priest, some of the congregation having converted to the RC faith the previous year. Long noted for its charitable work, Holy Cross now houses in its crypt a drop-in centre for vulnerable people. In 1982 the English Collective of Prostitutes staged a lengthy occupation the church after eviction from premises nearby. The east wall of the church displays colourful mosaic-style murals, which can be inspected at close range by entering the attractive 'garden of peace', created at its foot by the Cromer Street Garden Association.

Running just north of an old track leading westward from Gray's Inn Lane to the Boot tavern (p 93), the street was developed in 1801-15 by Joseph Lucas, a tin-man (or tinplate worker) of Long Acre, who had inherited 7 acres of cow pasture in the northern half of Peperfield. Originally called Lucas Street, it became so disreputable that by 1828 it had been renamed, probably after the Norfolk fishing village. His relationship, if any, to the East Anglian Lucas family at Nell Gwynne's Cottage (p 94) is unclear.

William Fletcher, said to have been valet to Lord Byron, was an early resident of Cromer Street. Here he set up in business making drain-tiles, partnered by two Italian brothers called Lambelli, and employing technology long used in the latter's homeland for the extrusion of macaroni. The radical Henry Vincent was arrested on 7 May 1839 at his home in Cromer Street. The warrant from the Newport magistrates charged him with having participated in 'a riotous assemblage' held in that town. He was committed to Monmouth gaol to stand trial, but so great was the tumult outside the court that the mayor was obliged to read the Riot Act. Vincent was found guilty and sentenced to twelve months' imprisonment. The intense feeling among the Welsh miners about Vincent's treatment in prison helped spark an armed rising of the Chartists in South Wales.

After heavy damage in WWII, little survives of old Cromer Street. No trace remains of the Baptist chapel existing here in 1839-68, of the LCC's Cromer Street School, or of the hall of the London City Mission at No.59. From 1931 to 1933, when it was wound up, this was the home of the National Minority Movement. The British Delegation Committee to the European Workers' Anti-Fascist Congress also used the address at this time. Gone too are the terraces of houses and shops which once lined the street, the Silver Cup pub (predating 1838) which failed to survive WWII, and the Marquis of Wellesley, which did not even make WWI.

Cross over to the north side of Cromer Street and pause again. Today, on the south side, set at right angles to the street and separated by lawns, is a series of balconied, brick-faced, 6-storey blocks of the late 1940s designed by Robert Hening and Anthony Chitty. Like their blocks for Holborn Council (p 16), these won the commendation of Pevsner, who liked their symmetrical arrangement. Their appearance has changed dramatically since 1995 in an imaginative refurbishment of the whole estate by Camden Council. While **Northiam House** (to your immediate right) is arbitrarily named after a Sussex village (see p 108), the other block names are of local historical interest. **Chadswell,** the next block along, recalls the former nearby spa (p 84); **Great Croft** was an earlier name for Peperfield, the field beneath our feet; and **Hollisfield** was the area developed as Argyle Square. The two easternmost blocks are **Mulletsfield**, recalling Thomas Mullett, proprietor in the 1790s of Bowling Green House (p 93); and **Peperfield**. This field name may have derived from 'peppergrass', an old word for 'cress'. The area was noted in the 18th century for the watercress that thrived beneath the elmwood pipes of the New River Company. These crossed Joseph Lucas's land on the surface, leaking profusely. The Harrisons and the Foundling Hospital had both refused to allow them to be laid over their property, but Lucas had obliged.

Running north off Cromer Street are four short, narrow, sloping streets. The layout survives from the initial development in the late 18th century, but the houses degenerated into slums and have not survived. Although most of this area, despite its reputation, appeared on Booth's poverty map in pale blue (for "mixed"), these little tributaries were shown in black, denoting "vicious, semi-criminal". Here some houses were shared by five families, and many of the women scraped a living making artificial flowers. Slum clearance in the 1890s led to the erection by the East End Dwellings Co. (EEDC) of six 4-storey model dwelling blocks built around courtyards, with an experimental mixture of stairwell and balcony access; the balconies were floored with expensive York stone. Four newer blocks were added along the Cromer Street frontage in the 1930s. Many of the block names are unexplained, but were presumably of some significance to the company's directors. In 1987 Camden Council proposed demolition of four of the older blocks. After an outcry by residents, the properties were instead sold to the Community Housing Trust, and in 1998 the **Hillview Estate**, as it is now known, underwent a five-year programme of rehabilitation, with much input from a caring and vocal residents' association. Some original square-cut wrought-iron balconies have controversially given way to modern 'Juliet'- style replacements. The profusion of window-boxes is not new: in 1892 the EEDC set aside £10 a year for prizes to encourage window gardening.

On the west side of Whidborne Street (p 112) is **Whidborne House**, whose central courtyard replaced Brunswick Grove, a narrow, triangular and no doubt treeless yard. Passing 1930s **Moatlands**, walk east to the top of **MIDHOPE STREET** (originally Wood Street), where 1890s **Midhope House** (left) faces **Charlwood House** (right).

Beyond the newer **White Heather House**, halt again at the next turning, **TANKERTON STREET** (once Dutton Street). Here in 1818, William Caslon, then residing in Burton Crescent (p 97), pioneered the manufacture of gas, the first gasworks known to have been erected in the parish. Gas was conveyed to customers in pitch-lined canvas balloons, stretched upon hoops, an iron pipe with a burner affixed being inserted into the drum. In 1890, when several old buildings were being cleared for the construction of sewers, a well, 12 ft deep and 8½ ft in diameter, was discovered in Tankerton Street, full of coal tar. This was supposed to have been one of the pits dug by the proprietor to get rid of the waste liquid then considered to be of no value. The Imperial Gas Light and Coke Company bought Caslon's gas-works in Dutton Street as a going concern, keeping it in operation until August 1824, when it was closed after a fire. A ragged school for boys moved here from Compton Place (p 66) in 1855, and a National School for boys and girls stood on the west side by 1870. There today stands **Kellet House**, which under the Council's 1987 demolition plans would have been replaced by an open space to be known as Kellet Square. **Tankerton House**, on the east side, is fronted by the later **Edward Bond House**, facing Cromer Street, and named after the first chairman of the EEDC. Beyond the next turning lie **Sandfield** council flats, their name recalling the nearby Skinners' property (p 91).

We now turn left into **LOXHAM STREET**, where **Loxham House** is a 1948 rebuild. Turn left again beyond the block into the footway known since 1937 as **ARGYLE WALK**. Linking the northern ends of the four 'Hillview' streets, it was previously called Argyle Place, although labelled North Place on the 1871 OS map. The EEDC had wanted to name it 'Cromarton Walk', while locals preferred their own nickname of 'Plum Pudding Steps'. The path's undulating progress is interrupted by the occasional shallow step, with a more substantial flight at this east end; the original early 19th-century development was so cheapskate that nobody troubled to level the ground.

Follow the pathway westward, passing on the right 'Tankerton Works' at **No.12**, of Victorian origin and now offices of Haines Phillips, architects. Pause at the junction ahead. The footway continues ahead to meet Tonbridge Street (p 94). Here originally named Sion Terrace, it is now lined on the right by modern **Nos.2-6**, a branch of the homeless persons' housing charity St Mungo's Trust; and on the left by two small EEDC blocks, **Lucas House** and **Ferris House**. The Rev. George Ferris Whidborne made land available for the building of Holy Cross church. A vicar in Battersea, but a wealthy man, Whidborne was the nephew of (and probably heir to) one John James Spencer Lucas, whose fortune derived from whaling. The latter's relationship, if any, to either Joseph Lucas the tin-man,

or James Lucas the plasterer, is unknown.

We now turn right, along **WHIDBORNE STREET**, originally Brighton Street. This northern section was part of the initial development of former Manchester Street and still retains its early buildings. To our right at No.5 (once No.33 Manchester Street) is **McGlynn's,** yet another Irish 'theme pub', which was known until 1996 as the Duke of Wellington. The pub has expanded into the two houses at Nos.1&3 (No.32 Manchester Street), which on the 1871 census appears to have been a separate jug and bottle establishment. The area of the bar that lies over former No.3 is known as the barber's shop in memory of the hairdressers who occupied the site in the mid 20th century.

Facing the pub at **No.12** are two windowless buildings, used in the 19th century as a stable and coach house, with domestic buildings behind. Standing alone at the north end of the street is **No.6**, known to locals as 'the white shop' and for most of the 20th century a butcher's. A craft shop from the 1980s, it is now residential. Alongside are the crumbling remains of Argyle School's gates, with separate entrances for boys and for girls and infants. The school itself has turned its back on the street which gave it its name, and now faces Tonbridge Street. It was built on a triangular piece of land not wanted by the Panarmonion Company, let in 1832 to a

Golders Green farmer, whose 'St Pancras Dairy' boasted a cowshed 300 ft long.

Turning the corner, we reach the north-south section of **ARGYLE STREET** (see also p 105). Started in 1832, this has always been known by its present name. From outside the **Wardonia Hotel** look north towards St Pancras Chambers, the former Midland Grand Hotel, and experience a scene screened repeatedly in *The Ladykillers* (also p 85). This was supposedly the view from Mrs Wilberforce's front door, No.48, though her house was actually a mock-up specially erected off Caledonian Road 1½ miles away. Little changed today, the scene is still dominated by small hotels converted from houses of the 1830s. On the corner opposite, at **No.47** (once No.37 Manchester Street) was the London Female Preventative Institution Open-All-Night Refuge for girls who would otherwise be prostitutes on the street. It took in more than 31,000 girls from 1872 until after 1907, but in 1919 it was successfully prosecuted as a brothel.

Continue north towards the Euston Road, stopping at **No.11** on the right. Here at what was then No.38, the actress Violet Cameron (real name Violet Lydia Thompson) was born in 1862. She and her husband were befriended by Hugh Cecil Lowther, fifth Earl of Lonsdale, but were later divorced when she gave birth to a daughter, the child of Lonsdale. Now named Faith House, No.11 has long served

35   Reggiori's restaurant (from a souvenir brochure)

as a local base of the Salvation Army; 'midnight patrols', targeting prostitution, were still being made from here in 1974.

Backtracking slightly, turn left into **ST CHAD'S STREET**, originally called Derby Street, hence modern **Derbyshire House**, offices (in 2008) of Metronet Rail. Proceed across Argyle Square, to the street's eastern end. Here at **Nos.1-7** a few old houses of 1827-8 survive, technically 'third-rate' but with very ornate wrought iron balconies. At No.11 once stood the Globe public house, used c.1830 for meetings of the Battle Bridge Paving Board; it closed before WWI. Opposite is the **Margaret Hepburn Centre,** headquarters of Age Concern Camden. The adjacent garage access was once the 'Grand Entrance' of the Royal London Bazaar (p 89), where another fine Ionic portico was demolished long ago by Whitbread's.

Retrace your steps a few metres to **BIRKENHEAD STREET**, intersecting from the north. This was begun by Bray in 1825, and named Liverpool Street until 1938. Entry to its historical southern end is now barred by security gates, erected in 1996 as part of Camden's King's Cross Estate Action scheme. **Riverfleet** flats, within the fortress, mark roughly the site of the 'Royal Entrance' to the old Bazaar and the offices (at No.11 Liverpool Street) of the Panarmonion Company.

Turn north along the rump of Birkenhead Street, whose east side is lined by Bray houses, converted long ago into small hotels. Housed in the street in Edwardian times were the Female Preventative & Reformatory Institution and the Midnight Meeting Movement.

King's Cross Wesleyan Chapel opened on the west side of Liverpool Street soon after it was laid out. W H Smith (later of bookshop fame) was among the original trustees. The chapel was enlarged in 1865-6, with a mission hall facing Crestfield Street (p 103). Rebuilding after WWII reversed the arrangement, with the church facing Crestfield Street, and the church hall, now **King's Cross Methodist Church**, here in Birkenhead Street. In 1992, a Chinese Methodist Mission arrived at the church. Today, the Chinese congregation is thriving, and the church remains home to a small English-language congregation. Outreach work includes a local ecumenical project working with women in prostitution, and an advice service working with Chinese immigrants

No.61, Centra House, to the north, marks the site of a little theatre opened in 1830 as part of the Panarmonion scheme, and the only element of it to be completed. It was meant to be used for tuition and rehearsals, but was pressed into revenue-earning service when the parent project collapsed. It survived, precariously, for some 50 years, with several changes of ownership and eight changes of name, but is perhaps best remembered as the Royal Clarence or Cabinet Theatre. Polini and Edmund Kean were among the famous actors who trod its boards. The site was later absorbed into Reggiori's restaurant (**[35]**, p 113; see also p 102), the striking classical building picked out in blue and white which rounds the corner into Euston Road. 1997 saw the opening of a new 'Police Office' on the opposite corner, occupying an old branch of the Capital & Counties Bank. The Metropolitan Police had at last returned to King's Cross, over 150 years after deserting the base of the monument which once stood directly opposite, and which gave the district its name.

Sources

Books and pamphlets

Aston, Mark. *The cinemas of Camden*. LB of Camden, 1997

Aston, Mark, & Lesley Marshall. *King's Cross: a tour in time*. CLSAC, 2006

Barker, Felix, & Denise Silvester Carr. *Crime & scandal: the black plaque guide to London*. Constable, 1985

Barker, T C. *Three hundred years of Red Lion Square*. Camden Libraries, 1984

Bebbington, Gillian. *London street names*. Batsford, 1972

Booth, Charles. *Life and labour of the people in London*. 9v. Macmillan, 1892-7

Braithwaite, David. *Building in the blood: the story of Dove Brothers of Islington, 1781-1981*. Godfrey Cave, 1981

British Printing Industries Federation. *11 Bedford Row*. The Federation, 1995

Besant, Sir Walter. *London north of the Thames*. A & C Black, 1911

Central St Martin's College of Art & Design. *Plain, reasonable & well built*. The College, 2007

Cherry, Bridget, & Nikolaus Pevsner. *London 4: North*. Penguin, 1999 *(The buildings of England)*

Eyles, Allen, & Keith Skone. *London's West End cinemas*. 2nd ed. Keystone, 1991

Fairfield, S. *The streets of London: a dictionary…* Macmillan, 1983

Fitzhugh, Henry, & Rosemary Jeffreys. *56 Argyle Street: a sympathetic biography of our comfortable home*. 2005

Godber, Joyce. *The Harpur Trust, 1552-1973*. The Trust, 1973

Gordon, Edward, & A F L Deeson. *The book of Bloomsbury*. Edward Gordon Arts, 1950

Green, Shirley. *Who owns London?* Weidenfeld, 1986

Hair, John. *Regent Square: 80 years of a London congregation*. Rev. ed. James Nisbet, 1899

Hamilton, Godfrey H. *Queen Square: its neighbourhood and institutions*. Leonard Parsons, 1926

Heal, Ambrose. *The London furniture makers from the Restoration to the Victorian era, 1660-1840*. Dover, 1972

Hobhouse, Hermione. *Cubitt, master builder*. Macmillan, 1971

Holborn (Met. Borough). *Flat and furniture 1948, Dombey Street, Holborn, WC1*

Holborn (Met. Borough). *Official guide*. 1922, 1927, 1931, 1932, 1934, 1958, 1961

Holborn (Met. Borough). *Tybalds Close: the Holborn housing scheme*. [1960s?]

Holborn Chamber of Commerce. *Industrial Holborn and its many industries*. [1938]

Howard, Diana. *London theatres and music halls 1850-1950*. Library Assoc., 1970

Hunter, Michael, & Robert Thorne (eds). *Change at King's Cross, from 1800 to the present*. Historical Publications, 1990

Lehmann, John. *Holborn: an historical portrait of a London borough*. Macmillan, 1970

London County Council. *Opening of Kingsway and Aldwych by His Majesty …* 1905

McClure, Ruth K. *Coram's children: the London Foundling Hospital in the eighteenth century*. Yale U P, 1981

McGee, John Edwin. *A crusade for humanity*. Watts, 1931

Marchmont Street Association *The story of Marchmont Street, Bloomsbury's original high street*. 2008

National Hospital. *Queen Square and the National Hospital 1860-1960*. Edward Arnold, 1960

Nicholas, Messrs. *The Doughty Estate, Holborn WC, 3rd sale* [auction catalogue], 1921

Nichols, R H, & F A Wray. *The history of the Foundling Hospital*. Oxford U P, 1935

Osman, A P. *Pigeons in the Great War*. Racing Pigeon Pub. Co., 1929

Pepper, Peter. *A place to remember: the history of London House*. Benn, 1972

St George the Martyr Church. *St George's: celebrating 300 years in Holborn*. The Church, 2006

Summerson, John.
  Georgian London. New [4th] ed.
  Barrie & Jenkins, 1988
Survey of London, vol.24: *King's
  Cross and neighbourhood*.
  LCC, 1952
Tallis, J. *London street views 1838-40*
Tames, Richard. *Bloomsbury past*.
  Historical Publications, 1993
Weinreb, Ben, & Christopher Hibbert
  (eds). *The London encyclopaedia*.
  Macmillan, 1992
Whitley, W T. *The Baptists of London,
  1612–1928*. Kingsgate Press, 1928

Maps

Rocque 1746; Rocque 1769;
Horwood 1799; Thompson
1801/1804 (& terrier book); Davies
1834; Greenwood 1834; Britton
1834; parish 1849 & 1861; Cassell
1862; Ordnance Survey 1866-71 &
later; Bacon 1888; Booth's poverty
maps 1889–98; Goad insurance
maps; LCC bomb damage maps.

Compact disc

The Argyle Square sound trail. King's
  Cross Voices, 2006

Newspapers

Camden Journal
Camden New Journal
St Pancras Journal, 1947-1965

Articles

Antiquarian Book Monthly Review,
  vol.9 no.7, July 1982, pp 262-267:
  George Sims, "Alida Monro and
  the Poetry Bookshop"
Architects' Journal, 11 July 1996:
  "Scaled-down solutions"
Camden History Review, vols **2** 1974,
  pp 7-8 [Mrs Ward]; **9** 1981, pp
  4-9 [model dwellings]; **13** 1985,
  pp 15-18 [Parton St]; **15** 1988, pp
  15-19 [New Road]; **17** 1992, pp
  13-16 [Panarmonion]; **18** 1995, pp
  6-9 [coach-building]; **22** 1998, pp
  11-15 [WWII, Holborn]; **23** 1999,
  pp 13-18 [Lighthouse building];
  24 2000, pp 6-11 [Church of
  Humanity]; **25** 2001, pp 5-9
  [horse repository]; **28** 2004, pp 17-
  20 [British College of Health]; **31**
  2007, pp 19-21 [the Left in
  Gray's Inn Rd]

Country Life, 17 Apr 1937, pp lxxx-
  lxxxiv: "Old Devonshire House, 48
  Devonshire Street"
  Country Life, 30 Oct 1985, pp 950-
  951: Giles Worsley, "The saving of
  Dombey Street"
Georgian Group Journal, vol.**12**
  2002, pp 163-214: Richard Garnier,
  "Speculative housing in 1750s
  London"
The London Journal, vol. **29** 2004,
  No.1, pp 62-84: Isobel Watson,
  "Rebuilding London: Abraham
  Davis and his brothers, 1881-1924"
London Topographical Record, vol.**10**
  1916, pp 1-16: Philip Norman,
  "Queen Square, Bloomsbury and
  its neighbourhood"

Other records

Census returns, 1841–1901
Camden Environment, Development
  Control, and Leisure Services
  Committees: reports & agenda
  items
LCC/GLC street lists
Post Office London directories
  (Kelly's)

Registers of electors, St Pancras
  and Camden
St George the Martyr: Poor Rate
  books
St Pancras Met. Borough: rate books
St Pancras Vestry: minutes
St Pancras Vestry: Poor Rate books

Websites

Numerous Internet resources,
  including:
www.camden.gov.uk/cindex
www.camden.gov.uk/isted buildings
www.camden.gov.uk/planning
www.oldbaileyonline.org
www.ukwhoswho.com
Charles Booth Online Archive
Times Digital Archive
Oxford Dictionary of National
  Biography

Archive centres

British Library
Camden Local Studies & Archives
  Centre, including Heal Collection
Guildhall Library
London Metropolitan Archives

Index

Streets included in the survey are indicated in boldface, as are the main entries for these and other selected subjects;
* = illustration
PH = public house